Thomas Nozkowski

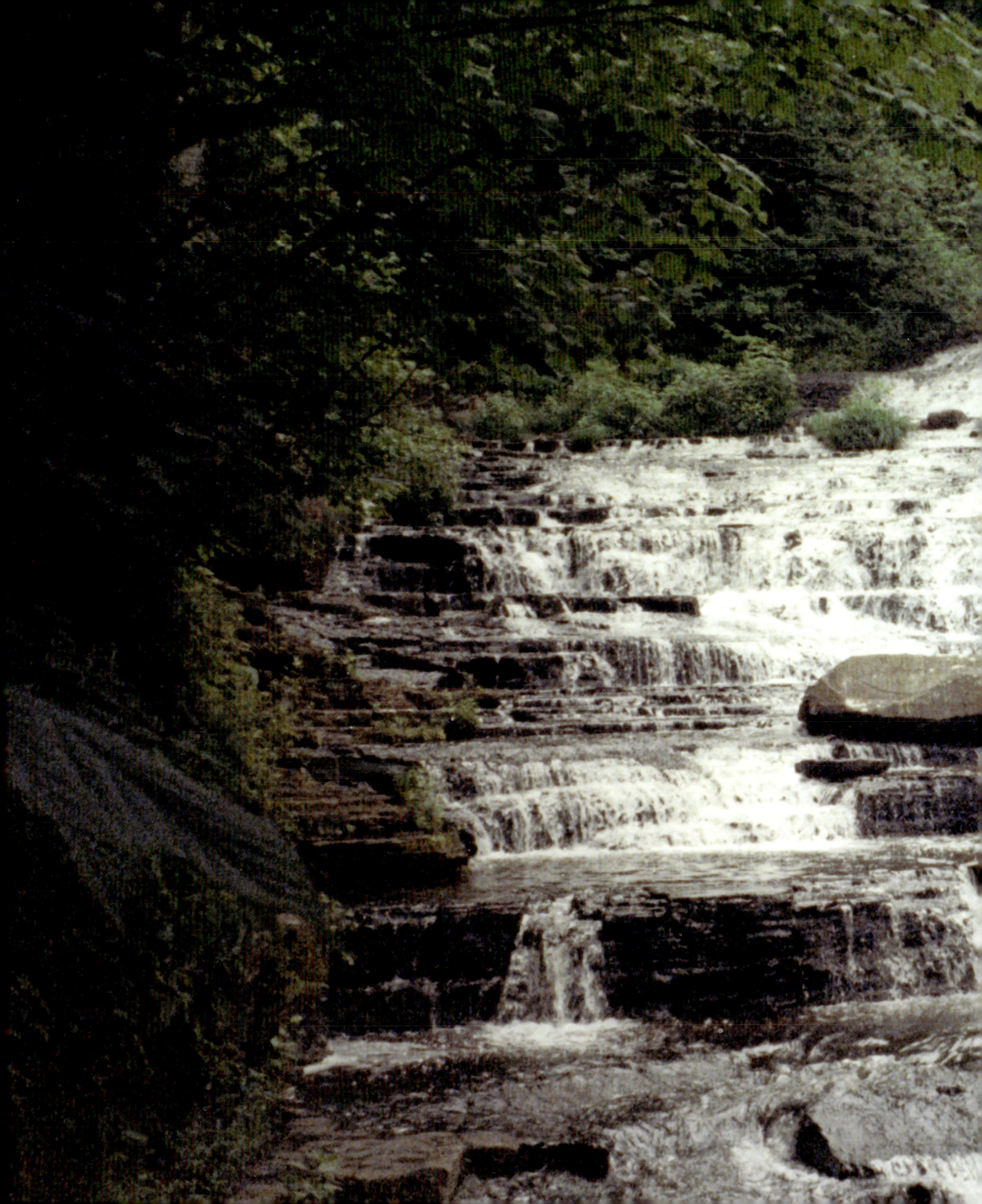

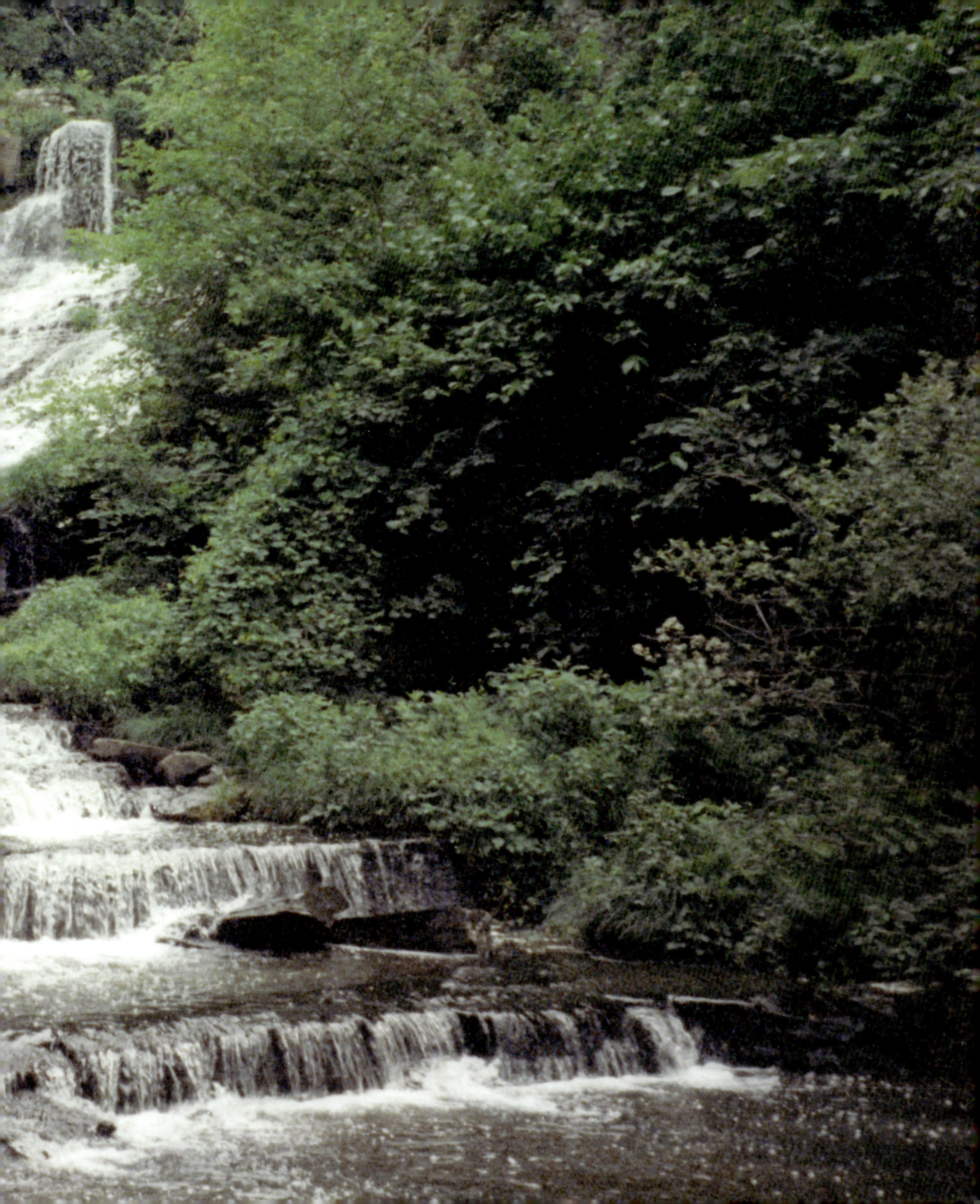

Previous spread: Rensselaerville Falls, Rensselaerville, New York
Photo by Thomas Nozkowski

Thomas Nozkowski

Everything in the World

March 8 – April 20, 2024

Pace Gallery
540 West 25th Street
New York

PACE

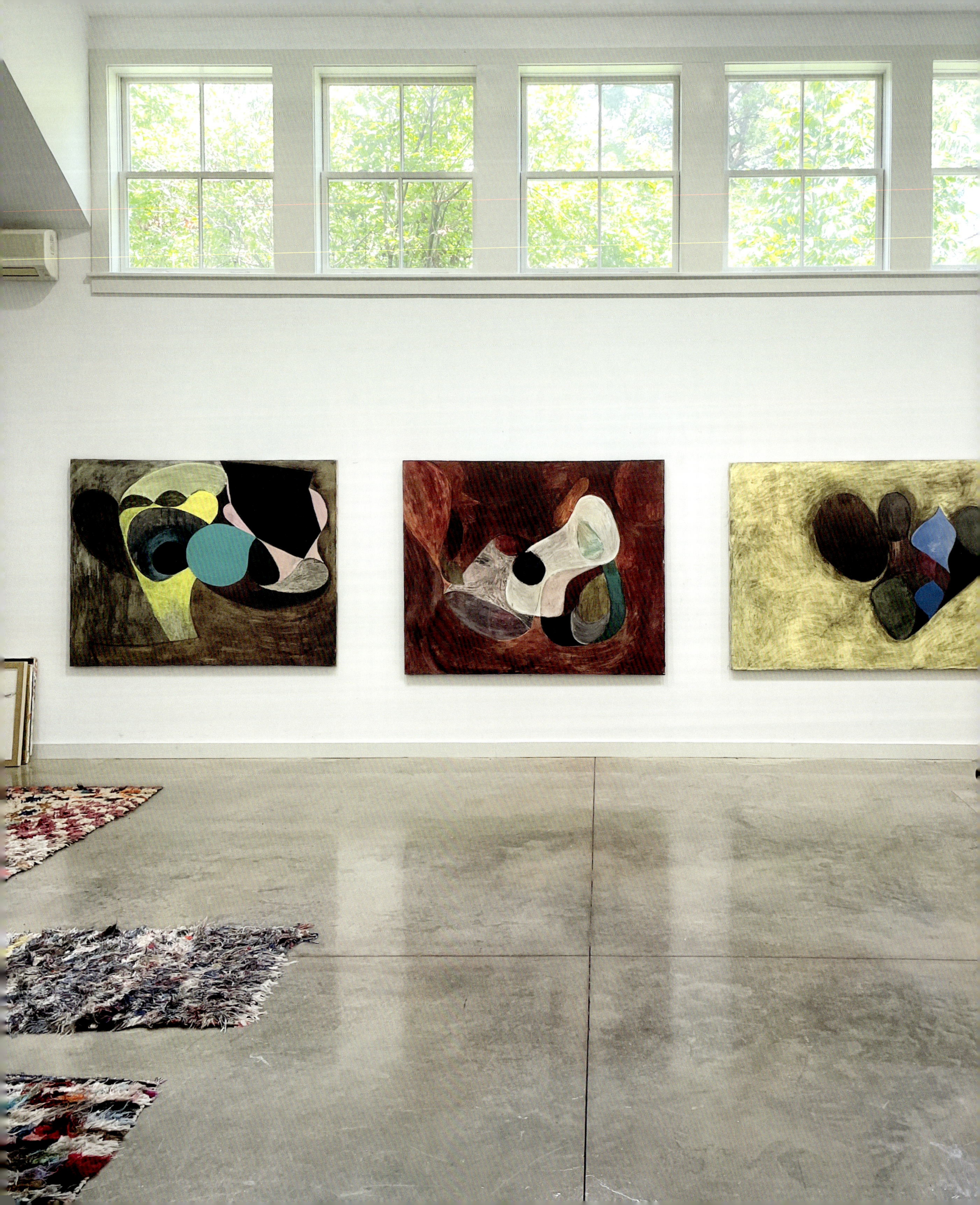

Introduction

Oliver Shultz

For Thomas Nozkowski the act of painting was like the act of thinking. To paint was to crystallize thought into form. A kind of dwelling or inhabitation, painting meant encountering the world, really *living* in it, beholding its splendor and its strangeness. To paint was also to confront the most profound questions about what it means to be alive, to embrace the riddles and the richness of everyday existence.

This exhibition catalogue marks Pace Gallery's third presentation of Thomas Nozkowski's work since his death in 2019 and the first posthumous show to focus on his early paintings. Centered on the late 1970s through the end of the 1980s, this exhibition explores Nozkowski's arrival at a mode of invention that would come to define him. His dedication to intimate, small-scale oil paintings—first on humble canvas board and then linen mounted on panel—remained unfailingly rigorous throughout his life. The exhibition also features never-before-exhibited paintings of a larger scale, all dating to 1986. At 4 by 5 feet, they are more than twice the size of his signature 16 by 20 inch format. These four magnificent outliers were equal parts fruitful and final. They mark an ending—or a denouement—but also a beginning: a turning point in Nozkowski's practice that saw him confront a set of questions that would prove enduring.

As curator and writer Martin Clark writes in his probing essay for this book, Nozkowski's idiosyncratic approach to painting was in fact rooted in sculpture. Clark cites the importance of what the artist called his "piles of matter"—early experiments with painted three-dimensional shapes. Nozkowski's art was indeed always deeply material, and the materiality of painting would prove among his most influential concerns, earning him reverence among the key abstractionists of his generation and after, from Martin Puryear to Amy Sillman. By painting not

Untitled (LP–4), *Untitled (LP–2)*, and *Untitled (LP–6)* installed in Nozkowski's studio in High Falls, New York.

“the thing … but the experience of it,” as Clark puts it, Nozkowski discovered a way to be fully engaged with the world. He was unafraid to let abstraction into the thick of life—where he located the sublime. His forms unfold to the rhythms and cadences of life in upstate New York, where he dwelled amid the forests, mountains, and rivers with his wife and son. Wildly complex yet astonishingly humble, his ideas about painting continue to reverberate powerfully today.

One can sense how Nozkowski’s project was born of a remarkable capacity to wonder at simple things. Heavily worked yet luminous, crudely physical yet ethereal, his paintings often feel more like alchemy than craft. Never content to make merely beautiful objects, each work is also a kind of philosophical investigation. Each confronts a new and specific problem at the root of things. Radically particular, yet containing whole universes, each one asks fundamental questions about the act of painting. What is a mark? What is surface? How can color be form and material? Line and life? Such questions animate Nozkowski’s process, leading him inexorably toward ever newer zones of experimentation. The resulting achievements of the 1970s and 1980s, at once ravishingly beautiful and intellectually penetrating, are testaments to this quest.

Pace Gallery is proud to present—in collaboration with Joyce Robins Nozkowski and Casimir Nozkowski—this seminal exhibition, which explores the roots of Thomas Nozkowski’s remarkable project and pays homage to his emergence as one of New York’s most important painters of the post-1960s era.

The Point of a Moment

Martin Clark

In my memory I may think I saw you but what I really saw was just a small piece of your face, the edge of the newspaper, the tip of my nose, a burst of sunlight. We know intellectually how much our visual memories are shaped by our culture and yet we still find it startling whenever we force the issue and really look at the world. The best things I've ever seen—my baby son, a beech forest in the fall, the city when I was seventeen—could scarcely be reproduced as I experienced them. We can never find the pictures we lived, but sometimes we can assemble a painting that can find clarity, the point of a moment, without denying its complexity and, yes, its confusion.[1]

—Thomas Nozkowski

At the beginning of the 1970s Thomas Nozkowski was trying to find a way out. Or perhaps it's more accurate to say he was trying to find a way through. Initially, though, it came from a refusal, it came from stopping one thing and starting something else. Tired of the legacies of Abstract Expressionism and the Bauhaus that he had been schooled in during the 1960s at Cooper Union in New York; alienated from the emerging currents of Pop, Minimalism, and New Figuration that were making waves in the galleries and institutions; and acutely conscious of the political climate of the time—the Civil Rights Movement, Feminism, Vietnam—he stopped making the paintings that he had "come to despise" and started making sculpture instead: "I just wanted out. Sculpture, or at least object-making, offered a line of escape." Although even sculpture was too strong a term for him back then. "Sculpture is a discipline and I wasn't having any of that either. Just object-making."[2]

These objects were often assemblages (see figs. 1 and 2). Or would he have pushed back against that word, too? Too highbrow, institutional, loaded? He referred to them as piles. Piles of things, piles of matter, piles of shapes, color, texture, and form: "rocks, glass, gravel, sticks, just about anything I could find in the woods or on the streets … stones, ceramic shapes, painted cloth."[3] Often arranged on the floor, occasionally strung up on wires and clotheslines, he showed them in a group exhibition in 1973 at Betty Parsons Gallery in New York. People liked them. In his words, he'd joined the "Painting is Dead club."[4] But that same year he found himself picking up his brushes again, initially working alongside the sculptures, but slowly, decisively, painting took over, and by the middle of the decade he'd found his way back.

He made two decisions at that time that would shape and inform the next forty years of his work:

> First I decided that my paintings would be small-sized and on canvas board, thus, by the taste of those days, rendering them unfit for any kind of institutional use. They were meant to hang in my friends' tenement apartments. Secondly, I decided everything I painted would come in some way from life. I would assume that you could do sophisticated abstract paintings that had touchstones in reality and I would act on that assumption.[5]

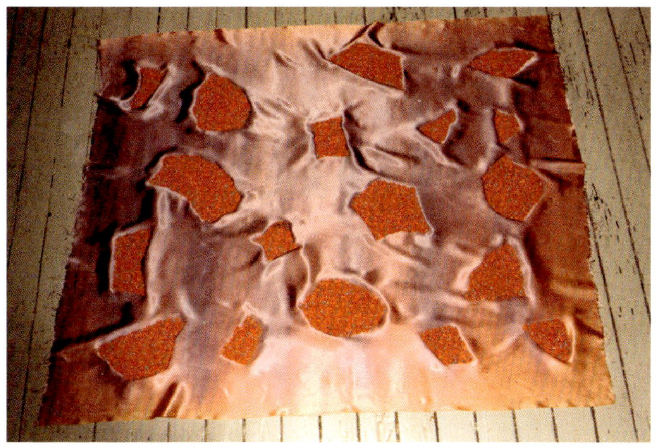

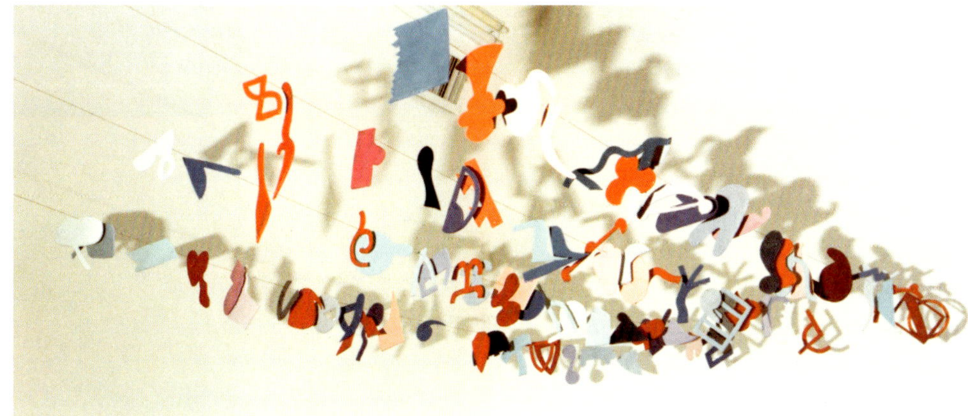

fig. 1

Thomas Nozkowski, *Untitled FS–1*, 1976, satin, reed, aquarium gravel

fig. 2

Thomas Nozkowski, *Hot and Cold Wars*, 1973, ceramic, copper wire

He settled on a format—16 by 20 inches—and the works he made during that period set the tone for everything that would follow: a determination not to be led by a signature style or movement, but instead by a way of looking and thinking about the world in its broadest sense. His approach to painting was driven not by grand ideas or overarching themes, but by a searching, curious, analytical engagement centered on our peculiar relationship and interaction with the world.

The size and scale of the work is one thing—we'll come back to that. But what does it mean to decide that everything he painted would in some way come from life? How could it not, we might reasonably ask. If you read anything about Nozkowski's work, you read about how all of the paintings, however enigmatic, obtuse, or inscrutable they might seem, are drawn from some concrete experience or referent, some "thing" in the world. Numerous commentators have noted the artist's reluctance to disclose or discuss these sources, despite his insistence that for him they are absolutely clear and present. He spoke many times of the fact that the starting point for his works might come from his beloved walks in the Shawangunk Mountains in New York State or in the city of New York itself, from an arrangement of objects he might glimpse in a room, or from a film, book, work of art, or a song. No one encounter is privileged over another, but as importantly, all of these starting points are experiential, and all of these things are things in the most expanded sense. In a statement from 2002 Nozkowski wrote, "My project has been to make paintings that come from things in the real world. I mean things to be taken in the broadest way: objects, ideas, moments—and I mean real world to be taken as broadly, including both physical and speculative realities."[6] But we're getting ahead of ourselves, let's go back to that moment in the mid-1970s.

Untitled (2–94) was made in 1975 (p. 28). An orangey, rust-brown form flows across the left-hand side of the painting. Isolated against an apparently featureless green ground, it's hard to read somehow. More liquid than solid, more a "movement" than a thing. It seems to pour over an obliterated architecture or landscape, its structure and form delineated by the unseen terrain that gives it shape. *Untitled (2–57)*, made the same year (p. 24), is more complicated in some ways. Superficially at least there's more happening on the picture plane. A similar form again snakes across a section of the painting, this one looking even more like water—an almost childlike attempt at a description of the fluid rush of a river or waterfall. Curving and slipping across a heavy block of indigo paint—as flat and imposing as a rock face—it is interrupted by an awkward yellow shape sitting bluntly and almost comically on the lower edge of the canvas—an incongruous interloper. The whole composition is framed against an orange-brown ground, which encroaches at the edges just enough to set the thing up as a thing, or a collection of things, an object or encounter framed front and center, in a discrete but expansive painterly space.

Over the next few years the "waterfall" motif appears again and again. Sometimes more explicit in its allusion to the real waterfalls Nozkowski would encounter on his frequent walks on the tracks and trails through Ulster County, sometimes pictured as a more ambiguous presence—a force or energy describing elusive, cryptic shapes, figures, forms, and affiliations. And what a perfectly simple, complete, complicated, and complicating thing a waterfall is. And what a perfect thing to think through Nozkowski's singular approach to his work and the world.

We all understand what a waterfall is, as an image, an idea, an entity—but what *exactly* is it? For millennia, it has been used as a motif in various cultures and mythologies as a symbol of the irresistible flux, flow, chaos, and turbulence of time, history, and life itself. It's also come to symbolize a place of mystery and enchantment, a portal or gateway to hidden realms, a site where the veil between two worlds opens up. Like a river, a waterfall is as much an "event" as something tangible or material. It's made up of various forces and fields, all acting and interacting on elements, materials, substances, and objects. It's a compound thing. A composite thing. But more than anything it's a process.

In his most recent book, *White Holes* (2023), the Italian physicist, Carlo Rovelli, suggests that, despite appearances, as we get ever closer to an understanding of the true nature of reality, the idea of things, objects, stuff, is merely an illusion.

Instead reality, including all matter, is really nothing more than a set of relations, interactions, processes, and correlations. Things, in and of themselves, do not exist, only the relationship between things. Another way of thinking or saying this is to assert that everything is a process, everything is an event, everything is formed through interaction, correlation, and change. It's a staggering and beautiful idea, revealed through the workings of the quantum world at the tiniest scales of reality, but mirrored also in the philosophy of ancient Greek and Eastern thinkers like Anaximander, Empedocles, and Nagarjuna. And what follows, is that *we* are a fundamental and intricate part of these relational processes too. It is our own intersection with the world which produces it, and produces us:

> We always make the mistake of thinking of ourselves as different from the world around us, of thinking that we are looking at it from the outside. We forget that we are like other things—that we, too, are like the things we look at ... we creatures of thought and of emotion are this interweaving that is formed at the macroscopic level between ourselves and the world. We are not just social beings who live on relationships with other human beings, and biochemical organisms that burn free energy from the sun, in common with the rest of the biosphere. We are also animals endowed with neurons that are interwoven, thanks to these correlations, with other parts of reality.[7]

• • •

A digression: In 2019, Amy Sillman curated a display for The Museum of Modern Art in New York, as part of the *Artist's Choice* series (see fig. 3, p. 16). Sillman is a painter, whose work extends into drawing, printmaking, digital animation, zine-making, writing, and the occasional sculpture. She is also a teacher—as was Nozkowski. Titled *The Shape of Shape*, the exhibition included a painting by Nozkowski, and was accompanied by a new edition of her long-running zine, *The OG*, with an essay by Sillman, "Further Notes on Shapes":

> A couple of years ago, I realized that I barely knew anything about *shape*. I didn't even know where to begin reading about it, aside from a few books on still life and one on the psychology of

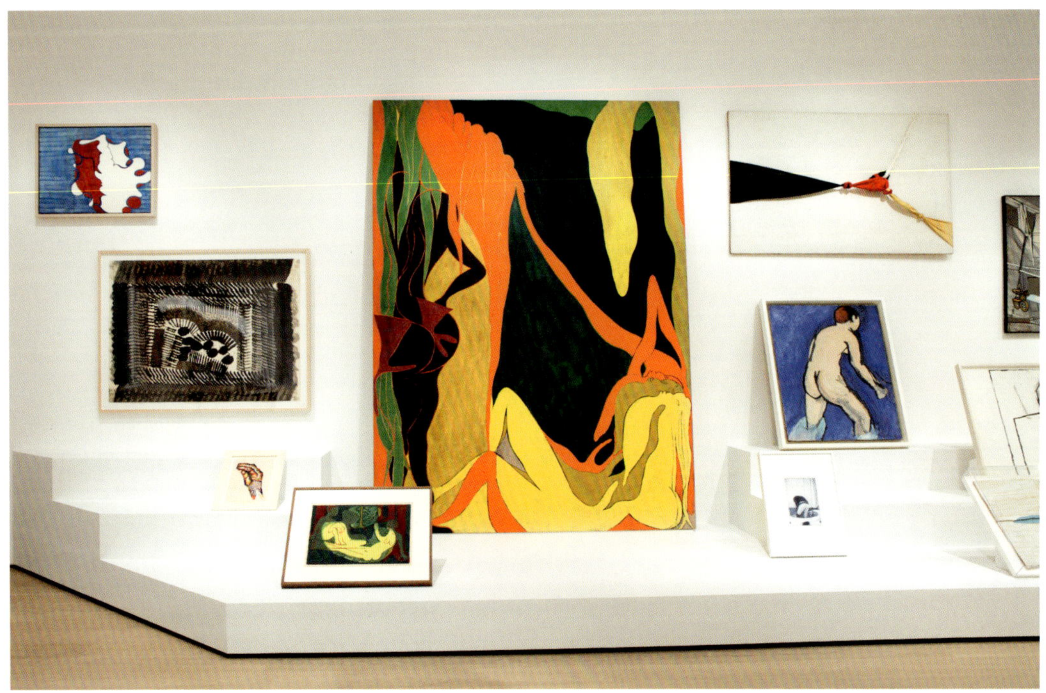

fig. 3
Installation view, *Artist's Choice: Amy Sillman—The Shape of Shape*, The Museum of Modern Art, New York, October 21, 2019 – October 4, 2020. Top left: Thomas Nozkowski, *Untitled 8–19*, 2001.

> perception. This was odd, because shape seems as fundamental to vision as color … basically everything in the world is a shape. It's so mundane and so ubiquitous: every edge, corner, blob, form, silhouette, or negative space is something you have to navigate to get through a room. If you think of shape as figure/ground, then every shape is a figure and the ground is the whole world.[8]

Up there with Hans Arp, Henri Matisse, and Frank Stella, Nozkowski is the epitome of a "shape-y" artist in Sillman's terms. And then there's that lesser known "alt-canon"—a "roster of artists' favorites" that might include Myron Stout, Prunella Clough, Jim Nutt, Christina Ramberg, Richard Tuttle, and Elizabeth Murray. But, she went on:

> For a long time I'd been nurturing a second idea, too … that you could divide artists into draw-ers versus painters.… Painters, it seemed like, work from an idea, moving deductively from the big picture down to the details in order to produce or construct an image they have in mind. Draw-ers, on the other hand, work from the weeds outward, building up from the particulars, inductively, scratching and pawing at their paper with tools the scale of their hand.[9]

Nozkowski is a draw-er in the most straightforward sense. Drawing was a fundamental part of his practice. He would often make studies of finished paintings as a way to revisit, rethink, and reengage with the work, and he always had a stack of "Stonehenge" paper next to him in the studio in case an idea, an image, a motif, or a passage needed developing or taking some place else beyond the canvas. But he is a draw-er in Sillman's more specific sense too: the paintings themselves "building up from the particulars," wiped away, worked, and reworked, worried at and over, coaxed and scratched and scraped and scribbled—agitated into existence. Their size reinforces this sensibility of course. Beyond the politics and pragmatics of that decision back in 1974 to work on these modest canvas boards, their scale also encourages a certain kind of engagement and concentration from the viewer, a very particular speed and style of looking. It calls to mind devotional paintings, medieval icons, antique manuscripts—a sense of reading the image as one might the page of a book.

• • •

> The right shape and the right color, the right scale and the right proportion, the right position and the right moment can make an event occur on a plane—an event that is as intense as, sometimes more intense than, anything in reality.[10]

By the mid 1980s, Nozkowski's work was moving away from the more linear, directional forms of the "waterfall" paintings. Where the works from the 1970s were almost calligraphic at times—a language or lexicon of often simple, diagrammatic forms, patterns, and pictograms—they gave way in the 1980s to a series of more geometric, organic compositions. In works like *Untitled (4–67)* (1983; p. 60) and *Untitled (4–120)* (1986; p. 64), shapes began to emerge which were somehow simultaneously more defined, more discrete, more "solid," whilst at the same time entangled in an increasingly dynamic and symbiotic relationship with their ground. Like the earlier works, many of these paintings have a strong relationship to forms found in nature. But rather than the rugged landscapes of the Adirondacks, or the implied description of terrains, topographies, and tectonics—the almost animistic bodies of water, rock, and natural totems Nozkowski would obliquely invoke—they picture instead more elemental, emergent structures—coalescing, clustering, and effervescing into existence. Some of these works seem almost representational, or as close to that device as he maybe ever gets. *Untitled (6–61)* (1988; p. 72) is strongly suggestive of a leaf and bud motif, others feel variously crystalline, geological, or evocative of biomorphic patterns and forms—of cells, amoebae, and botanical growth.

Around this time, Nozkowski also began working on a group of larger paintings, something he had done only very occasionally before. In a note from his journal dated May 28, 1985, he writes, "I spend the evening painting fairly well … I am getting ready to push some new large paintings." Then a week later, on June 5, "In the evening did some good painting on big canvas … feeling better about these big things in general. Also: during day Joyce phones Suzanne's stretcher maker and ordered me 6 48 × 60 stretchers."

Untitled (LP–6) and *Untitled (LP–10)* (both 1986; pp. 84 and 86), are two works from this series. In each, a loose pile of ovoid, pebble-like forms emerges from a ground that feels almost literally terrestrial. An excavation or unearthing, the shapes slipping over, into, and through each other—sometimes more solid, sometimes more amorphous or permeable, but nested in a heavy, burnished expanse of paint that holds them like a bedrock. Whilst the surface of Nozkowski's painting is always at least as important for him as color, shape, and line, in these larger canvases the grain of the work feels even more pronounced. He has spoken in interviews of always using small brushes, including for these larger works, recalling Sillman's description of her "draw-ers": "scratching and pawing … with tools the scale of their hand." There's a searching, restless quality to these works, building up and clearing back, exposing layers, strata, seams of color and texture—each field, form, structure, and void flickering with information and energy.

And where those earlier works from the 1970s recall the visionary, gnostic paintings of an artist like Forrest Bess (see figs. 4 and 5), whose own works emerged from vivid and hermetic dreams and hallucinations (and, like Nozkowski's, were often also expressed through an idiosyncratic lexicon of initially unfamiliar forms and figures, drawn from the light, shapes, and landscape of the remote Chinquapin Bayou near the Gulf of Mexico, where he lived and worked), these later paintings, superficially at least, seem closer to the languages of mid-century Modernism, and particularly European artists like Paul Klee, Vassily Kandinsky, or William Scott. In fact, a number of Nozkowski's paintings from this time call to mind a peculiar strand of British Modernism, developed in another rural idyll—this time the rugged coastal landscapes of St Ives in Cornwall where artists like

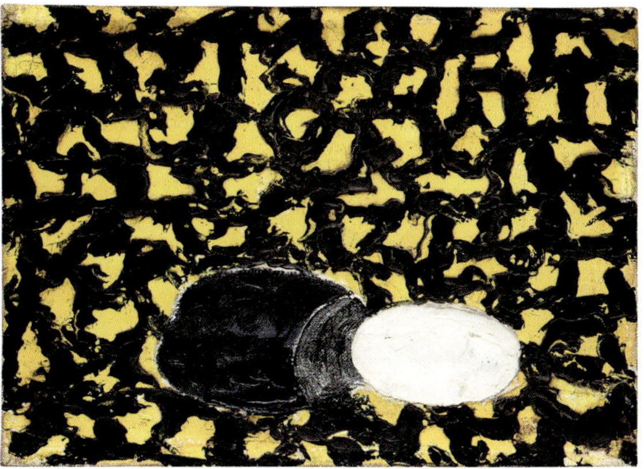

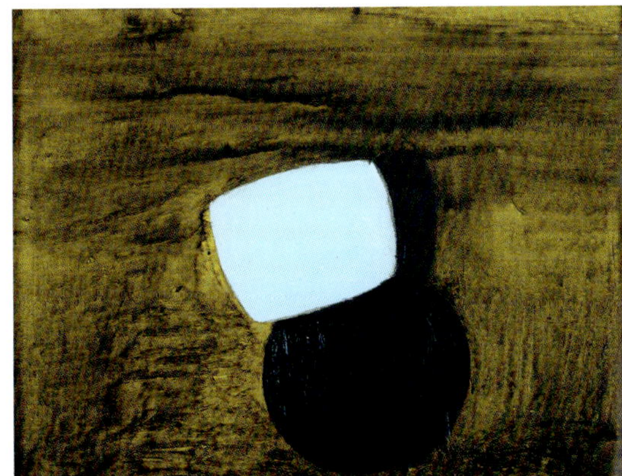

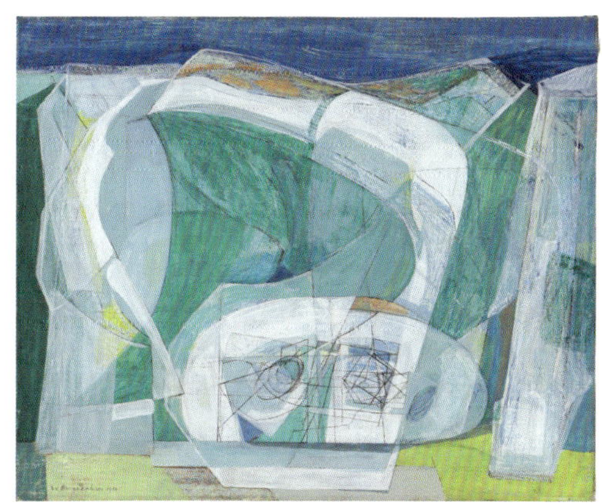

fig. 4

Forrest Bess, *It Fits*, 1955, oil on canvas, 6 × 8 ⅛"

fig. 5

Thomas Nozkowski, *Untitled*, 1981–82, oil on canvas board, 15 ⅞ × 20"
The Museum of Modern Art, New York

fig. 6

Wilhelmina Barns-Graham, *Glacier Crystal, Grindelwald*, 1950, oil and graphite pencil on canvas, 20 ¼ × 24"
Tate, London

Ben Nicholson, Barbara Hepworth, and Naum Gabo had fled to escape the Second World War. In the years that followed, a loose school of painters grew up around them, including Wilhelmina Barns-Graham, John Wells, Peter Lanyon, Margaret Mellis, Sandra Blow, and Patrick Heron, all of whom would draw on the natural forms and patterns they found in the landscape there to develop a language of abstraction, tied intrinsically to a sense of place (see fig. 6).

Much has been made of Nozkowski's own sense of place, his own "move to the country," when, in 1977, he and his wife, the artist Joyce Robins, bought their house in High Falls on the Shawangunk Ridge, building studios there for both of them. Throughout his life the connection with nature—through hikes and camping trips, taken both alone and with family and friends—was a fundamental and treasured part of his existence. But Nozkowski wasn't interested in abstraction as either a rarefied discipline of pure, idealized forms, set apart but somehow parallel to "nature," or as a way to produce a painterly language that operated as a kind of stylistic or gestural elaboration of the natural world. Despite his own unwavering insistence on a referent in the world, Nozkowski's paintings operate in an entirely other way. Tied to ideas of landscape, less for what they "picture" than for how they emerge into the world, they are not so much paintings *of* nature but paintings *as* nature—with nature understood now not as a narrow and reductive typology or genre, but as an expansive expression of the way the world produces itself, *for* itself, in all its impossible complexity.

. . .

> You know, when I say thing in the real world, we all imagine our thing. It's a craggy oak tree on a hill in a field or something. And for me, it becomes more interesting when the thing that I'm

> starting with is more complex, more ambiguous, endowed with lots of qualities of cause, of time, of space. And in fact, as I get older, I find it more interesting to go after evermore complex things.… I really wanna go as deeply as I can … as far as I can … and I guess that's part of what really interests me, which is how much we can see. How much we can think about what we can see. How big we are … and not about how small we are.[11]

We all make our own worlds and carry them with us, produced, moment by moment, through our peculiar points of contact and correlation—a reciprocal, generative, and deeply creative process. But what we call reality is always a caricature, a superficial manifestation, blunted by our imperfect and limited senses, masking a deeper, occluded, more fundamental nature. From his earliest mature works made in the early 1970s, to his last ones made in the days before his death in 2019, Nozkowski's practice was as much about painting as process, as it was about painting as image or object. The important thing for Nozkowski was not to paint the thing, but to paint the experience of it. To paint the way it acted upon him, and upon the world.

Nozkowski's world was a world of mountains and architecture, trees and constellations, rivers and streets, streams and sky, Coke cans and Tintorettos, laughter and stories, memories and songs. But the paintings he made are not about recording or bearing witness to all of this, they're not about making a trace, leaving a mark, or trying to communicate, even. They're about finding a way to think and make *with* the world, not apart from it—a way to get close to it. Through this encounter something new emerges, something real and complete, something utterly exceptional, to be encountered again now on its own terms, as part of the world it draws upon and inhabits, a world which we can only glimpse, ceaselessly imagining itself at the scales of the very tiny, the very big, the very distant, and the impossibly close.

In 1972 William "Bill" Unruh, a physicist at the University of British Columbia, Vancouver, gave a lecture at the University of Oxford, in which he used the analogy of a waterfall to try and describe the speculative properties of a black hole. Attempting to model the almost unimaginable force of gravity rushing toward, and finally over, the "event horizon," he wrote, "Imagine you are a blind fish, and are also a physicist living in a river." The "waterfall" plunges at supersonic speed, and as a fellow fish is swept over, its scream will never reach you, the waterfall dragging the sound down faster than it can travel up. For "sound," he went on to replace "light," the fish representing a photon now, the black hole sucking space-time into the vortex at such a speed and intensity that the fastest thing in the known universe cannot escape. As you get closer to the center, time slows to a standstill. Information and space and light and matter are collapsed together—concentrated, compressed, stretched, and reformed, everything made unfamiliar and strange. A singularity emerges which, from our perspective, from our position out here, is held now forever. The image is fixed. An instant. An instance. Just one in an infinity of others, as incomparable and as commonplace as a leaf or a look. The point of a moment.

1 Thomas Nozkowski in a statement titled "Homely Abstraction" prepared in relation to "A Discussion about Abstraction with Thomas Nozkowski and Dana Schutz" held at The New Museum, New York, May 17, 2008.

2 "Thomas Nozkowski in Conversation with Garth Lewis," *Thomas Nozkowski* (New York: Pace Gallery, 2010), 10.

3 Ibid, 10.

4 Ibid, 10.

5 Ibid, 8.

6 From a statement by Thomas Nozkowski, September 2002.

7 Carlo Rovelli, *White Holes: Inside the Horizon* (London: Allen Lane, 2023), 123–24.

8 Amy Sillman, "Further Notes on Shapes," *Shapes: The OG*, vol. 14 (Spring 2020): 2.

9 Ibid, 4.

10 Nozkowski statement, September 2002.

11 From a recorded conversation between Thomas Nozkowski, Andrew Hibbard, and Viola McGowan, held on February 4, 2015, at Pace Gallery, 32 East 57 Street, New York, 5th floor viewing room.

WENT TO FLEA MARKET, & A FEW ANTIQUE STORES. BOUGHT 1 BOOK FOR 1 $. PAINTED IN THE AFTERNOON.... TOTAL SINCE I STARTED THIS GROUP: 10 PICTURES, OF WHICH 4 ARE DONE (2 ARE QUITE GOOD), 2 MAY BE DONE & 4 HAVE A WAYS TO GO.

JOURNAL ENTRY
Sunday, August 26, 1979

WORKED ON 1 CONE SCULPTURE IN MORNING

JOURNAL ENTRY
Thursday, October 11, 1979

LATE AFTERNOON ACTUALLY GOT STARTED ON PAINTING: TENT. ANOTHER WATERFALL & A PROPHECY/ANNUNCIATION. WORKED LATE INTO EVENING AFTER SUPPER

JOURNAL ENTRY
Saturday, July 26, 1980

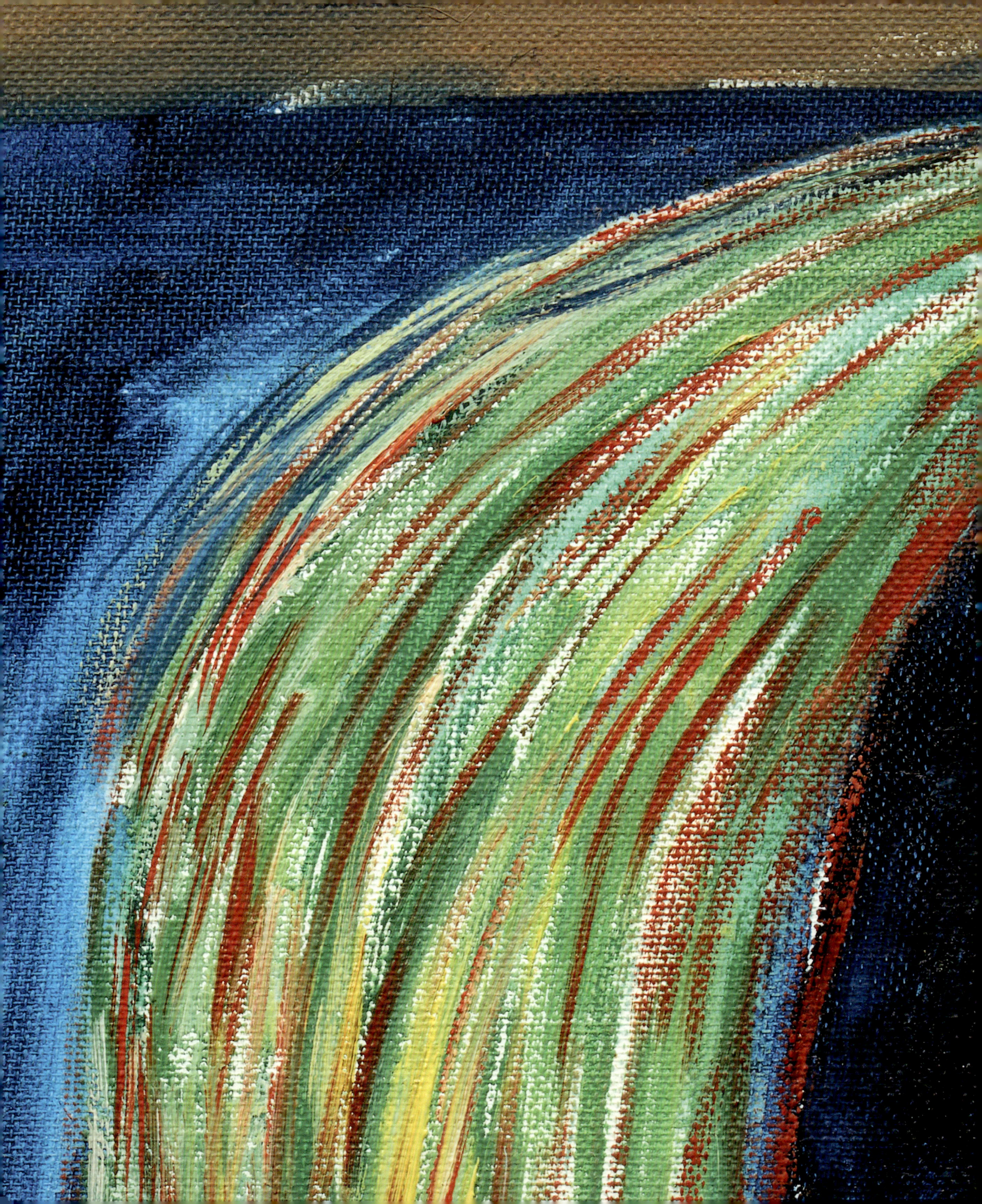

Untitled (2–57) 1975

oil on linen on panel
16 × 20"

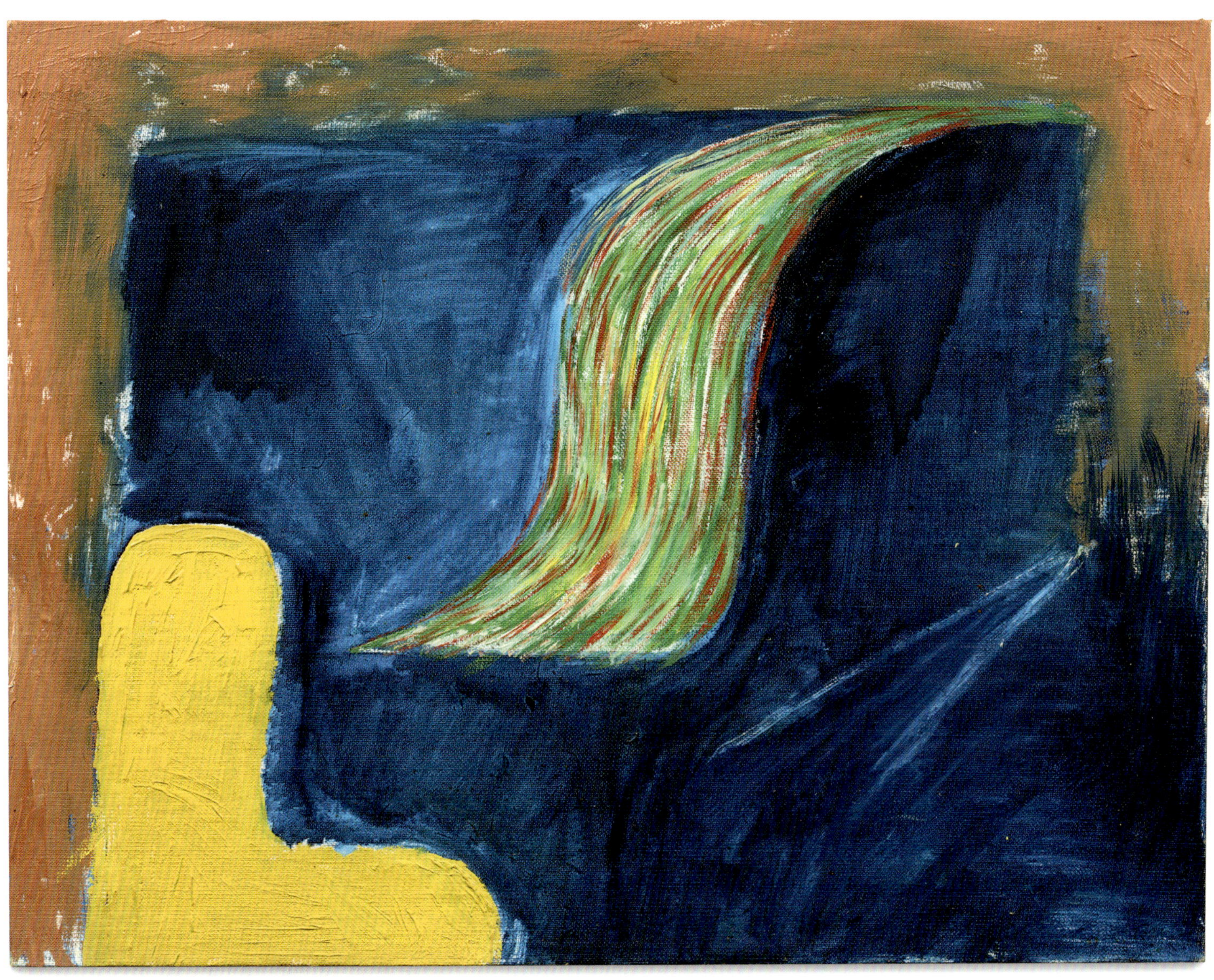

Untitled (2–92) 1975

oil on linen on panel
16 × 20"

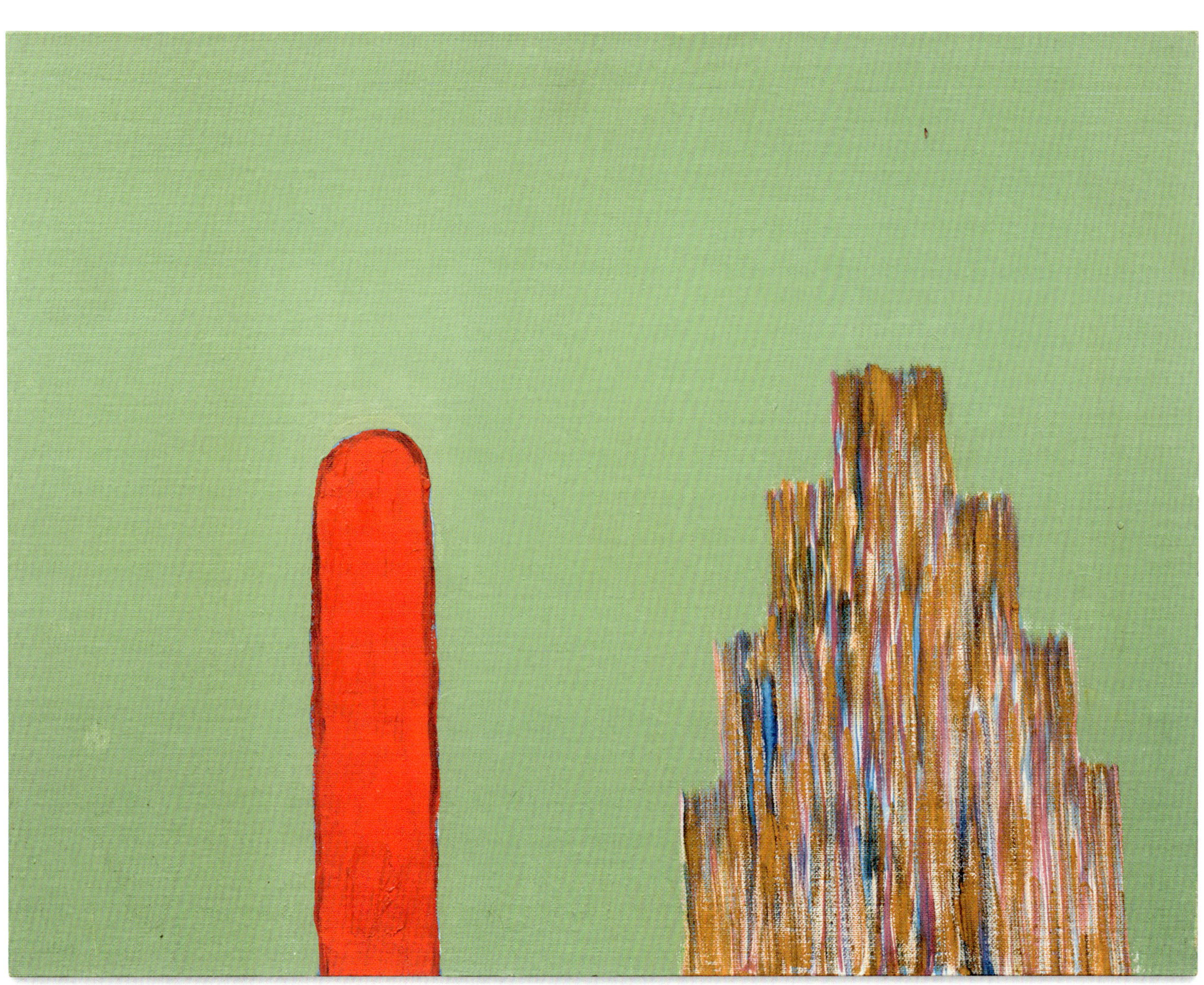

Untitled (2–94) 1975

oil on linen on panel
16 × 20"

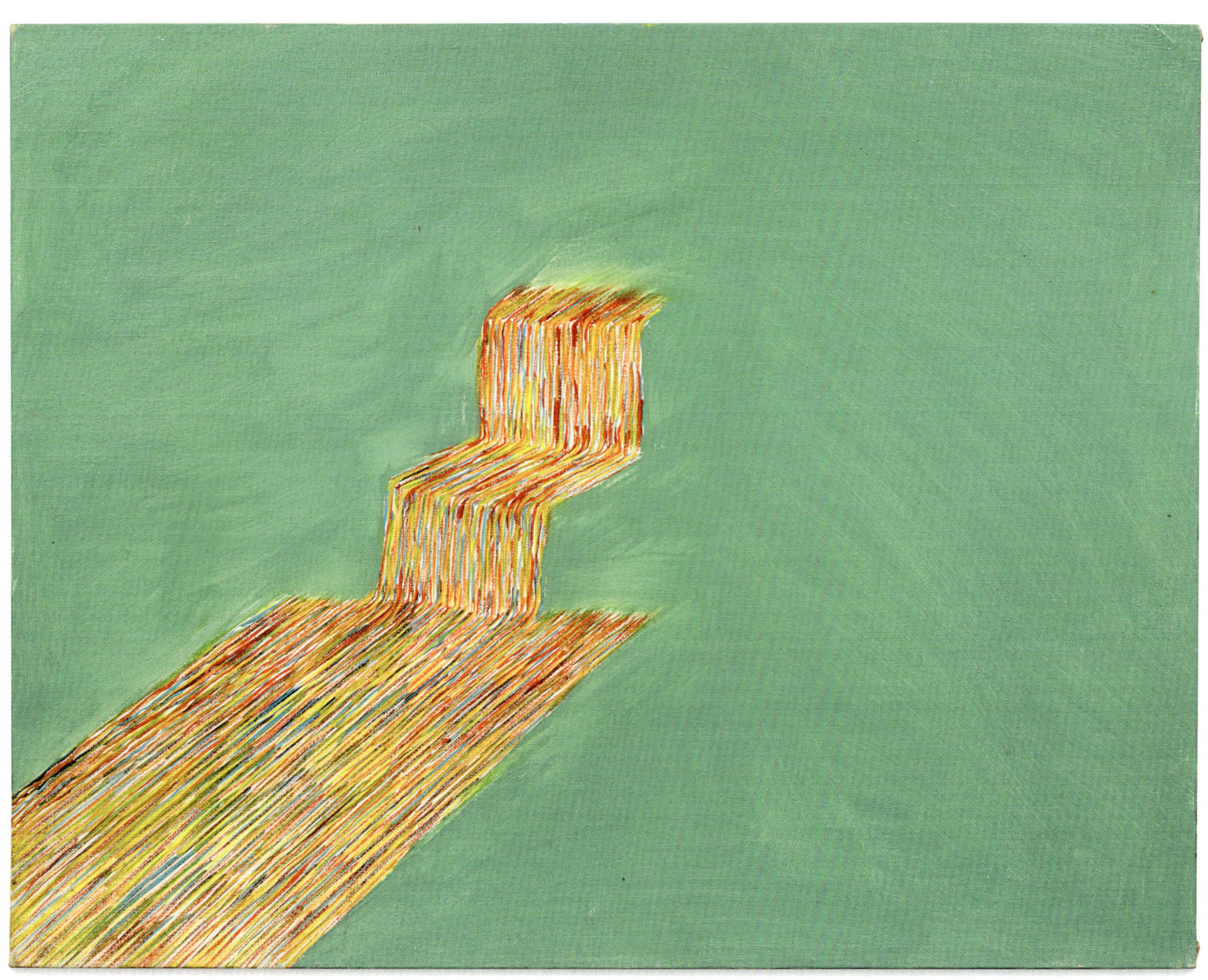

Untitled (I–II7) 1976

oil on linen on panel
16 × 20"

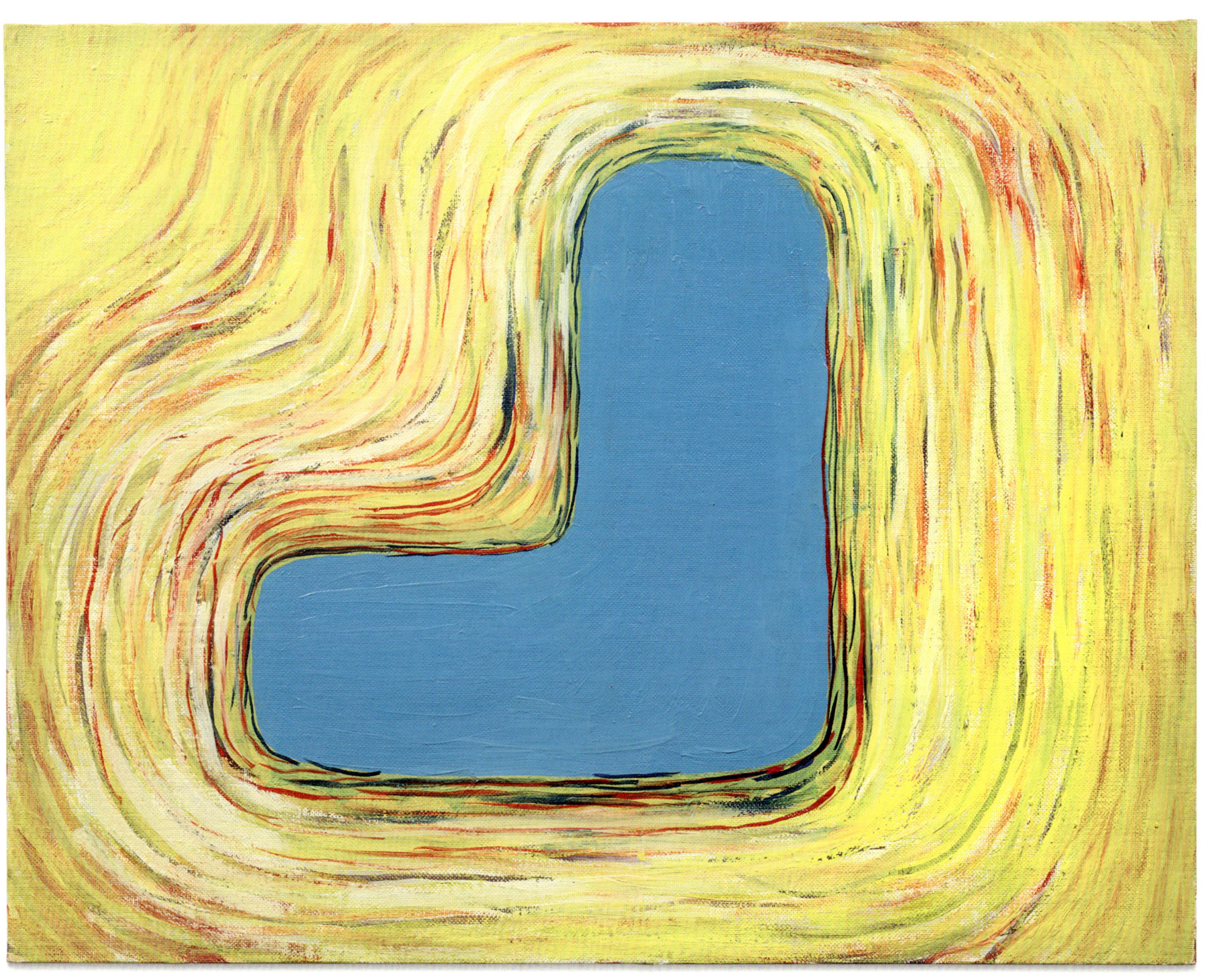

Untitled (1–120) 1976

oil on linen on panel
16 × 20"

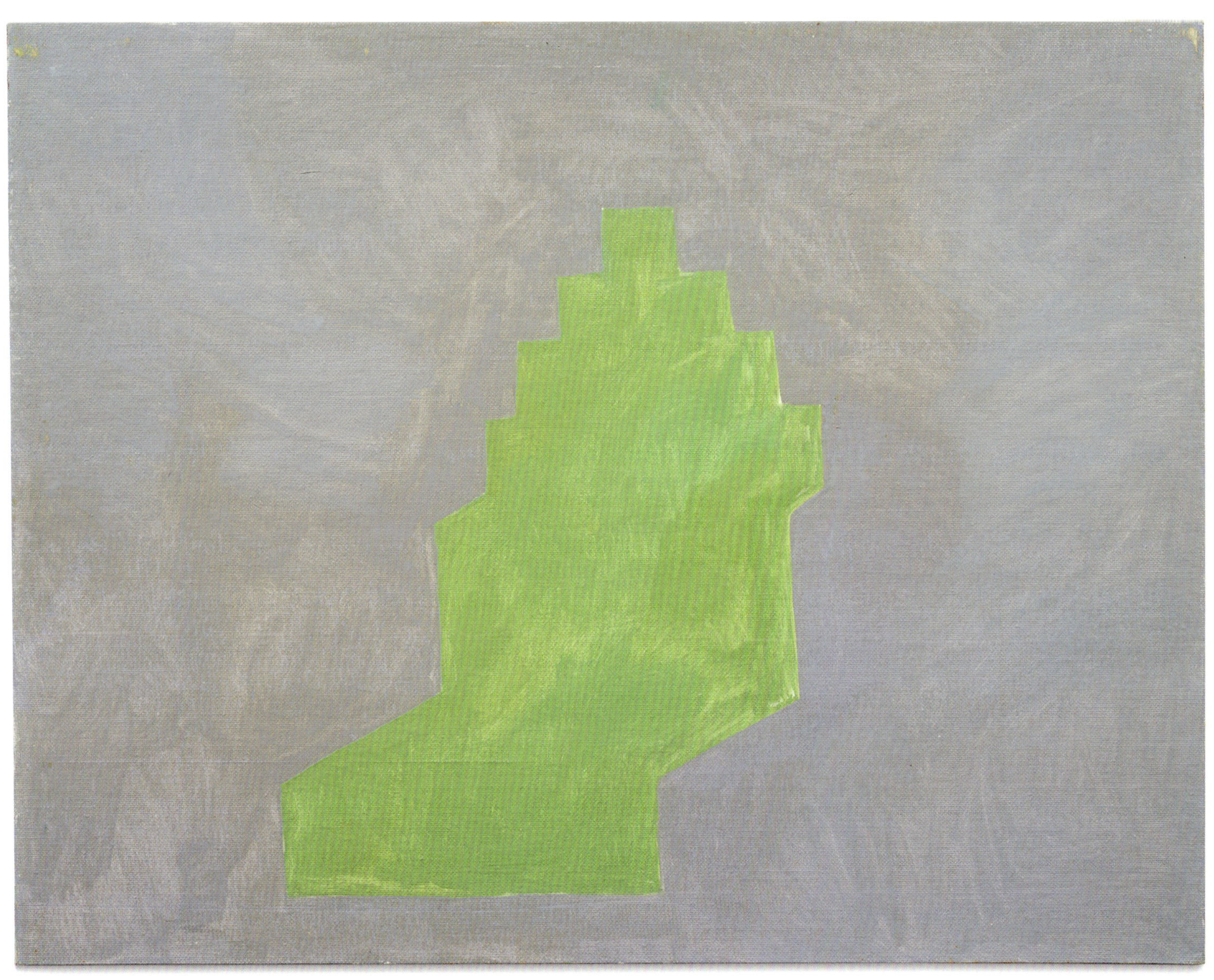

Untitled (2–44) 1977

oil on canvas board
16 × 20"

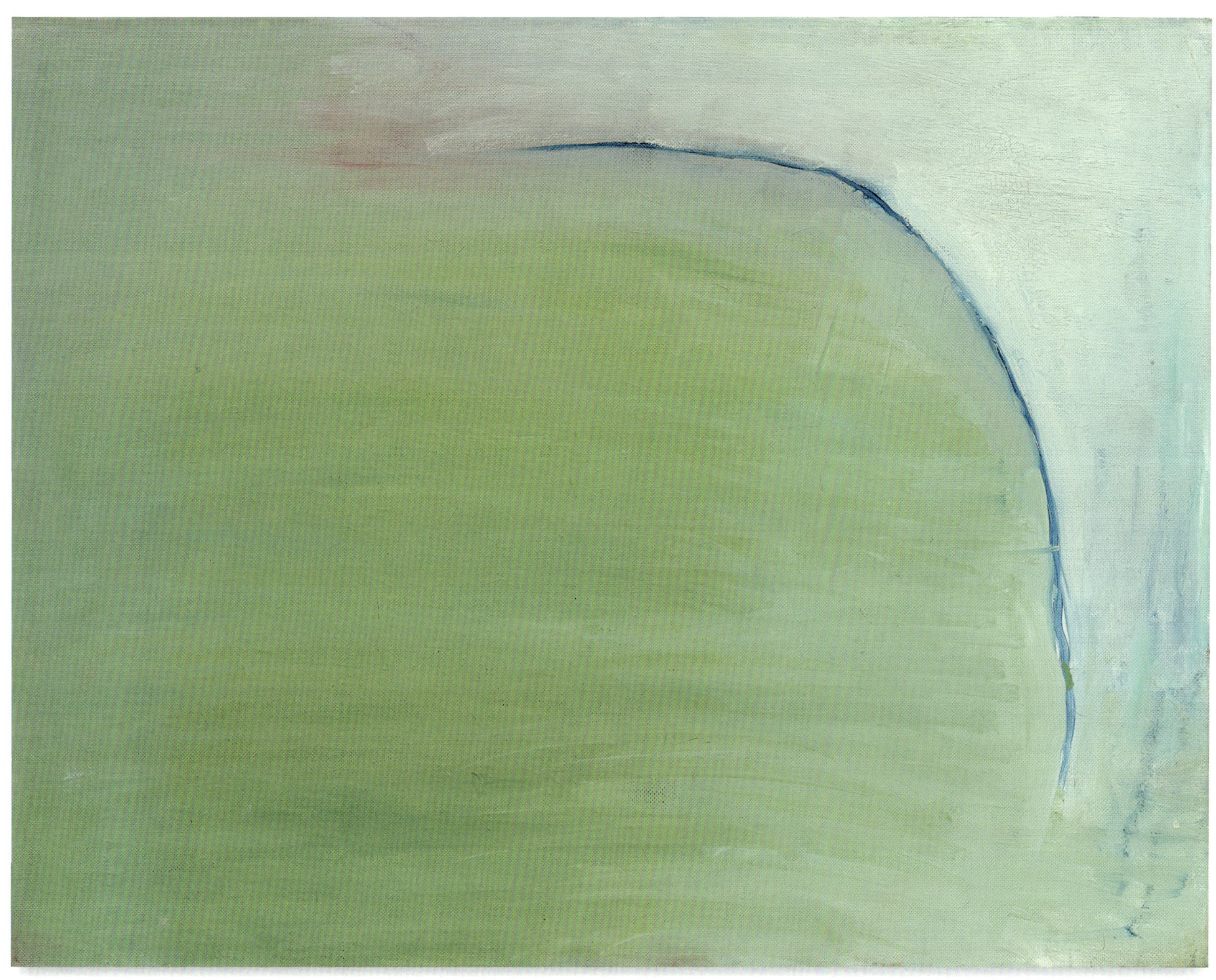

Untitled (2–58) 1977

oil on linen on panel
16 × 20"

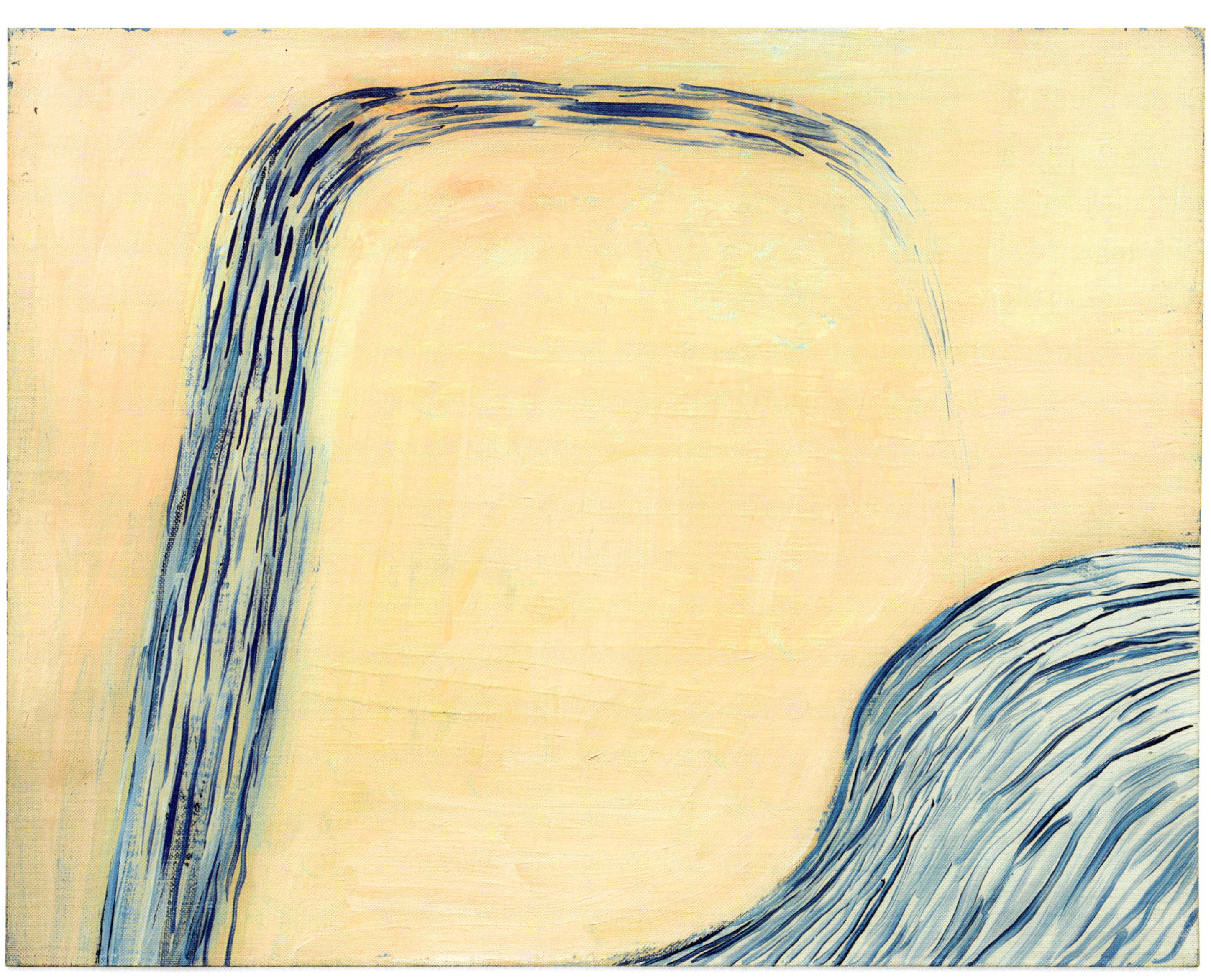

Untitled (2–62) 1977

oil on linen on panel
16 × 20"

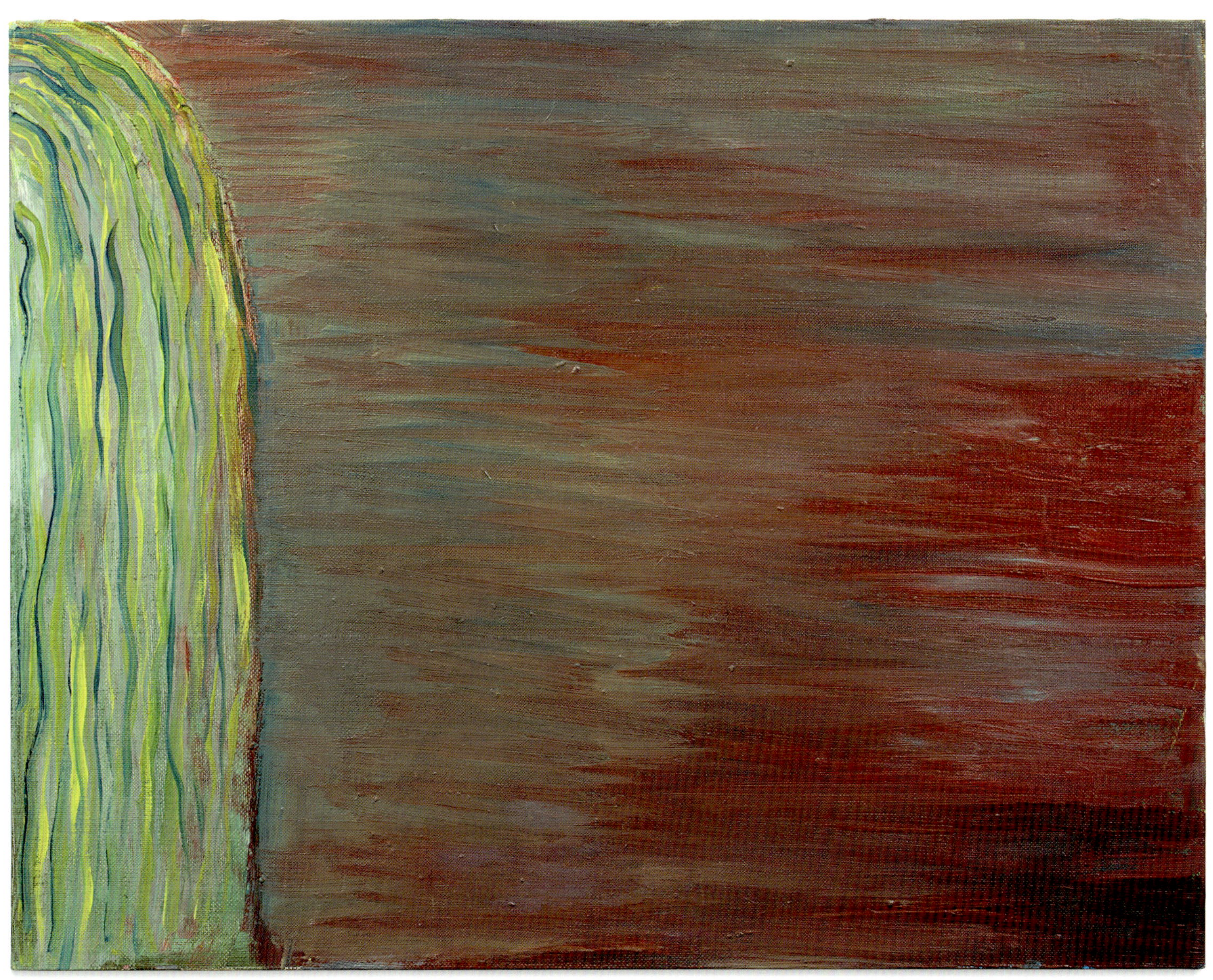

Untitled (2–72) 1977

oil on linen on panel
16 × 20"

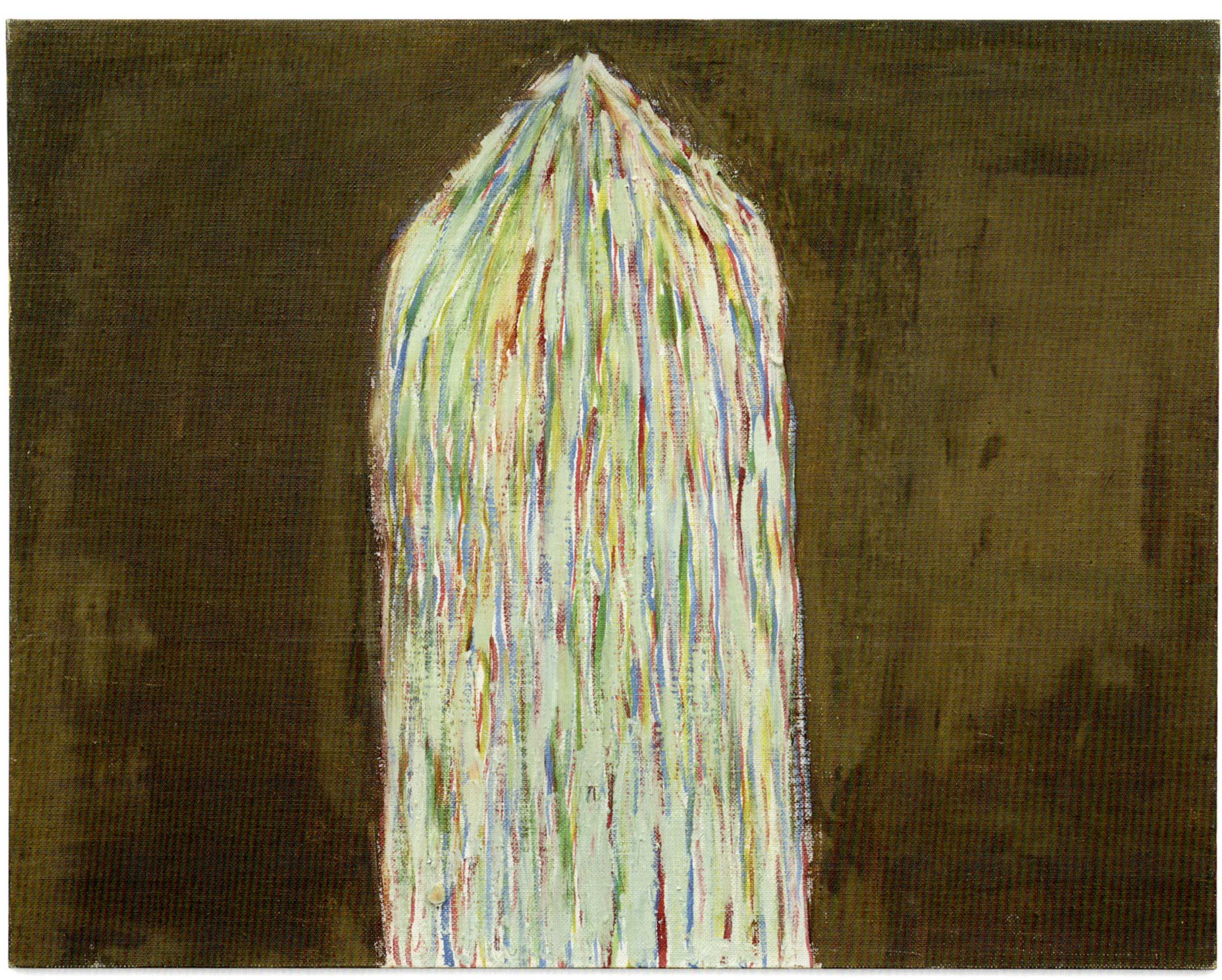

Untitled (2–110) 1977

oil on canvas board
16 × 20"

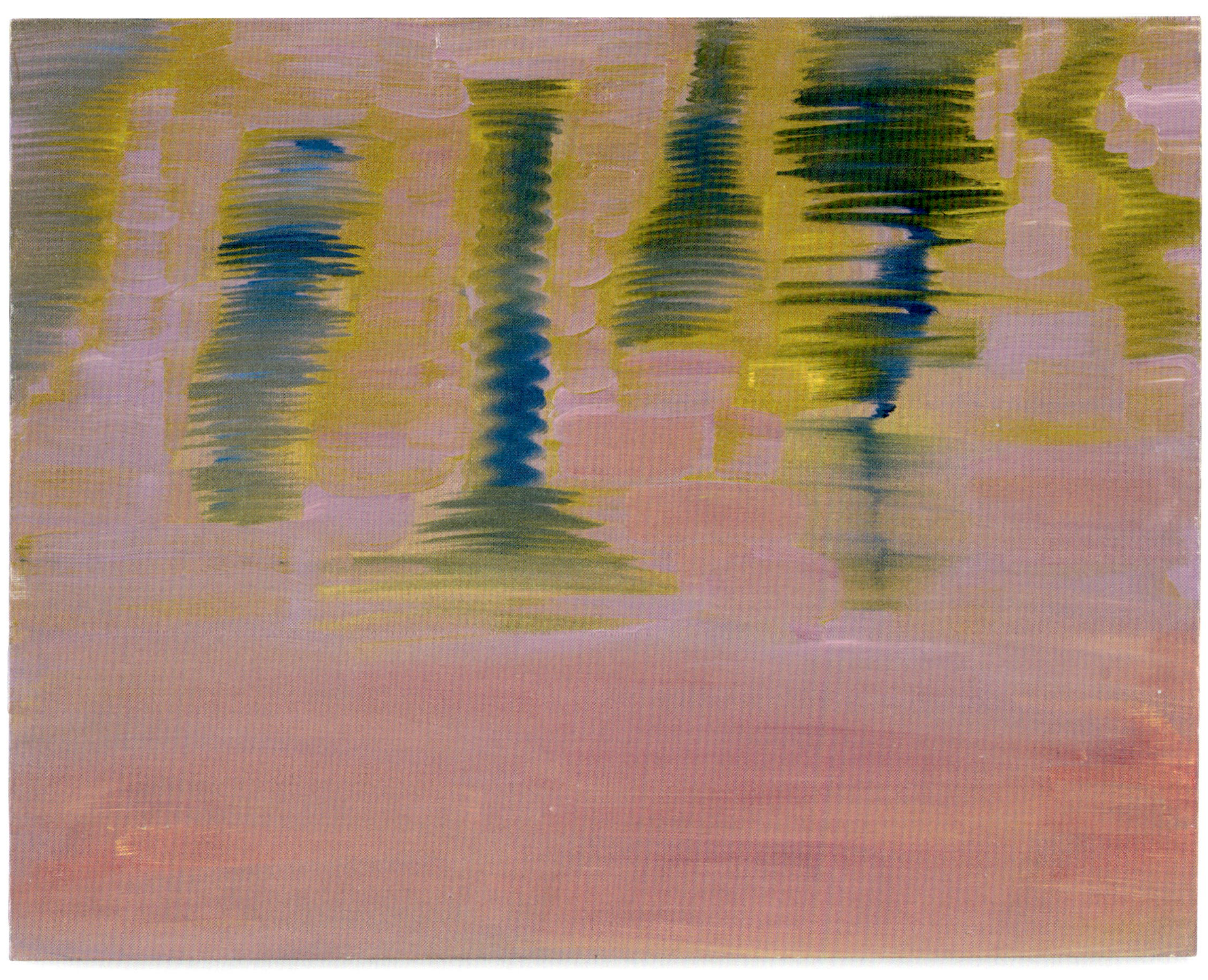

Untitled (2–59) 1979

oil on canvas board
16 × 20"

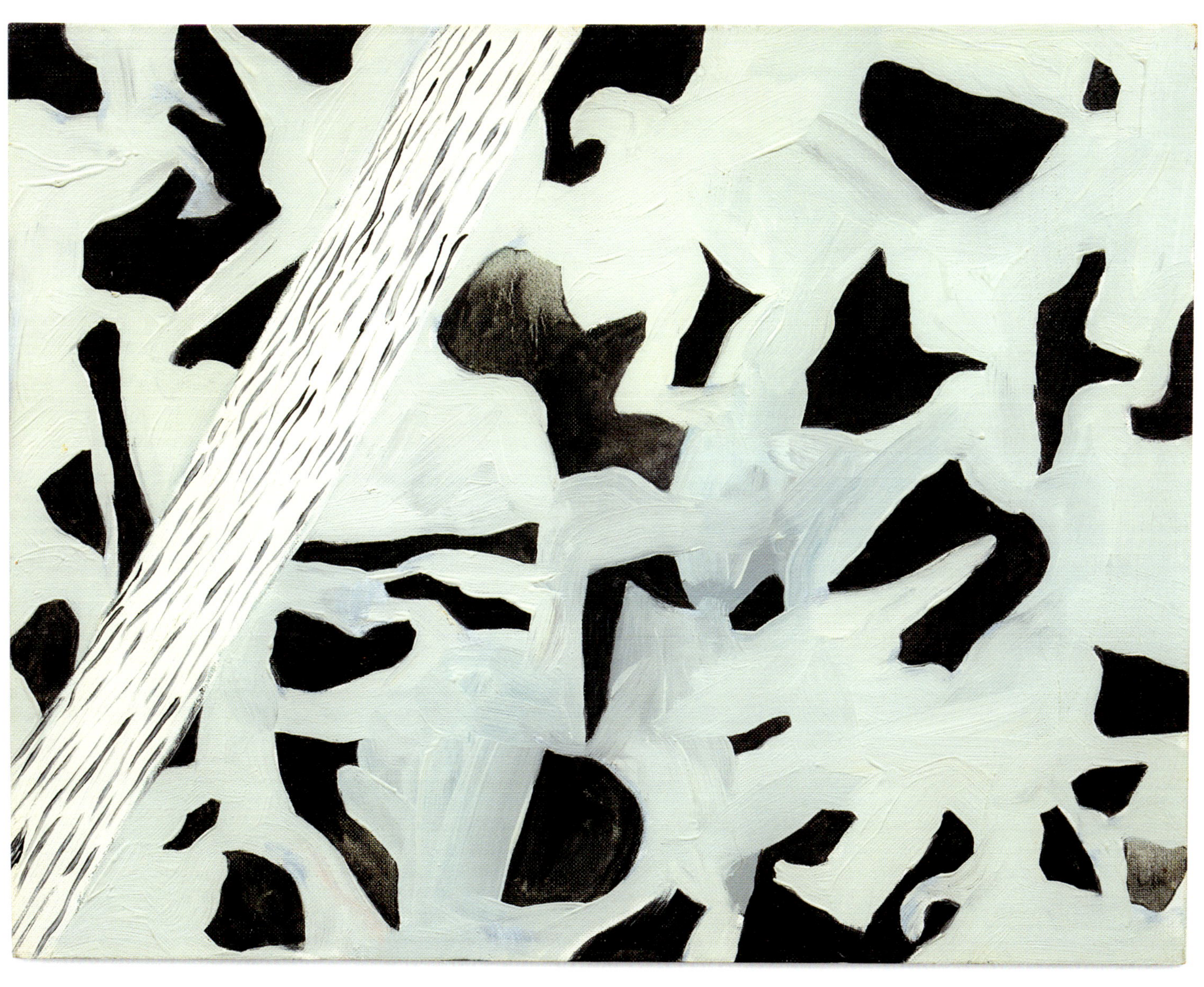

Untitled (3–12) 1979

oil on canvas board
16 × 20"

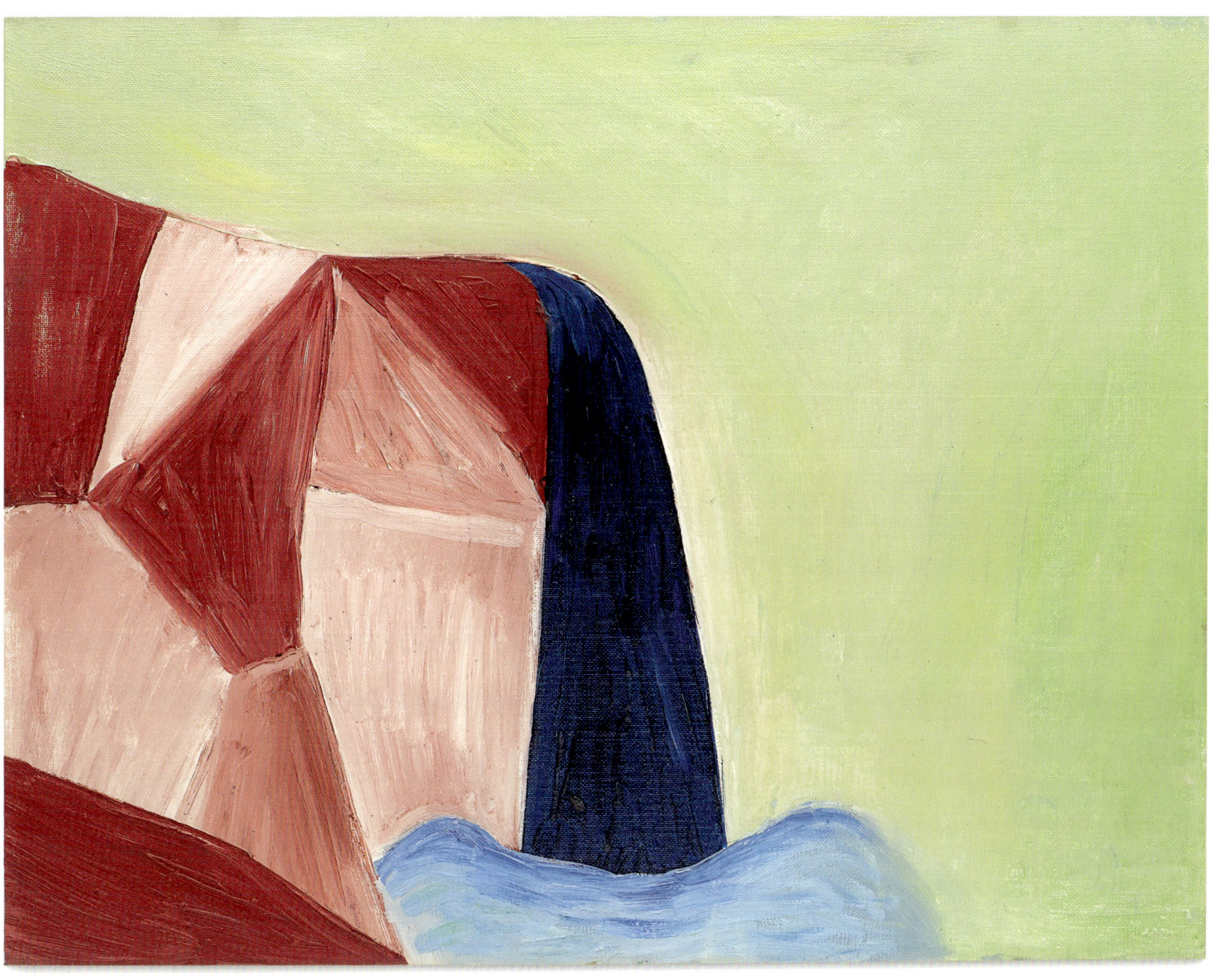

Untitled (3–28) 1979

oil on linen on panel
16 × 20"

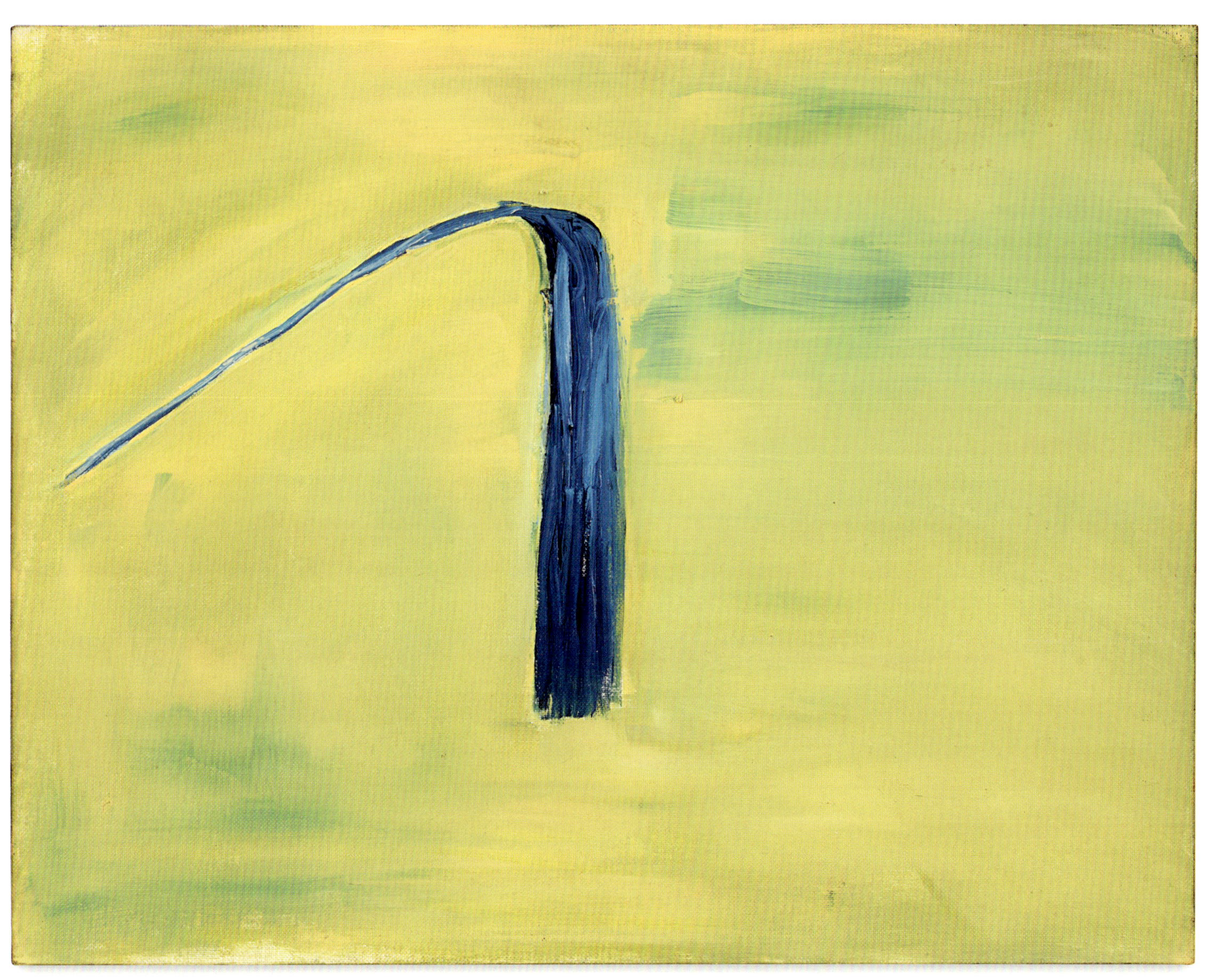

Untitled (2–78) 1980

oil on linen on panel
16 × 20"

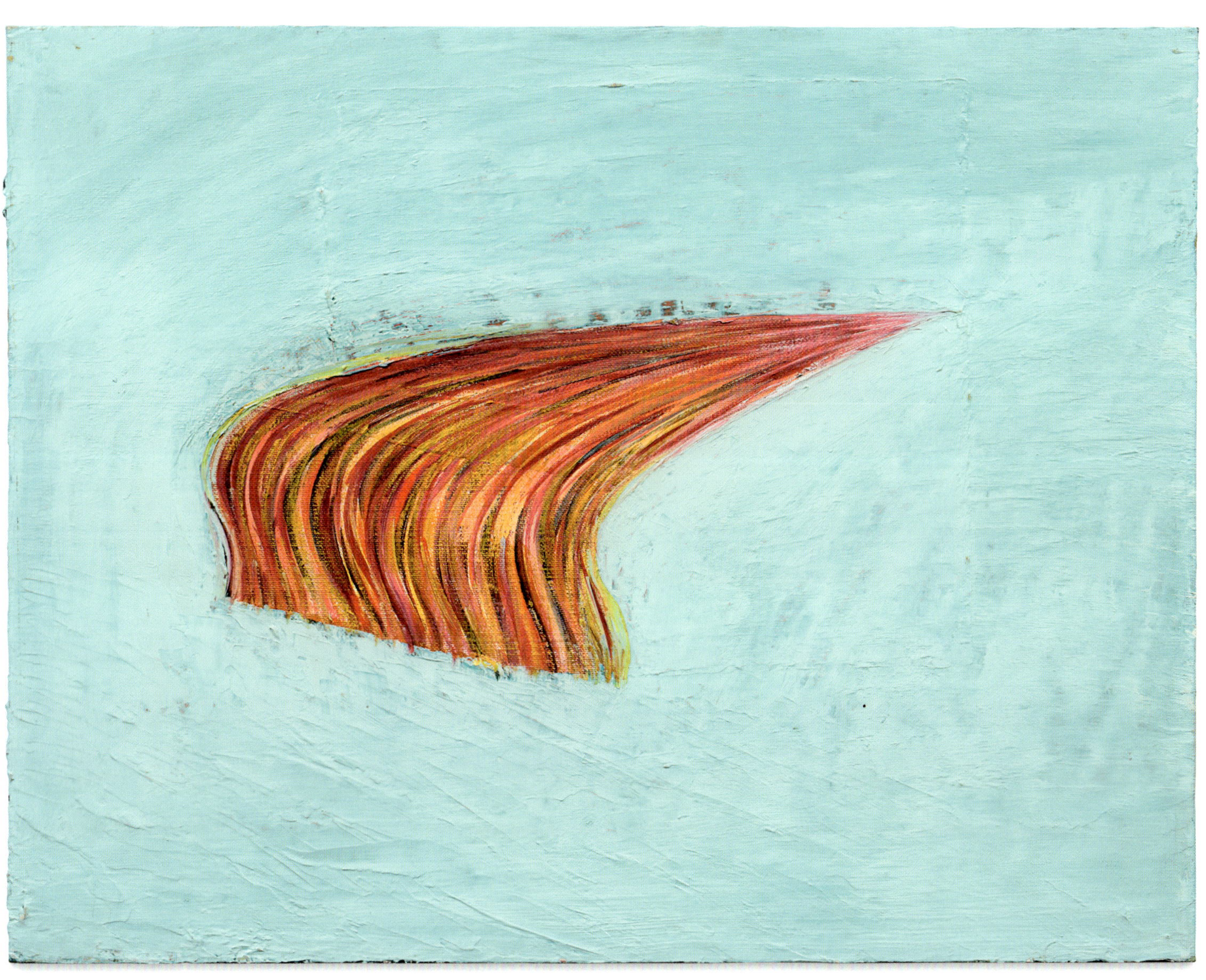

Untitled (2–101) 1980

oil on linen on panel
16 × 20"

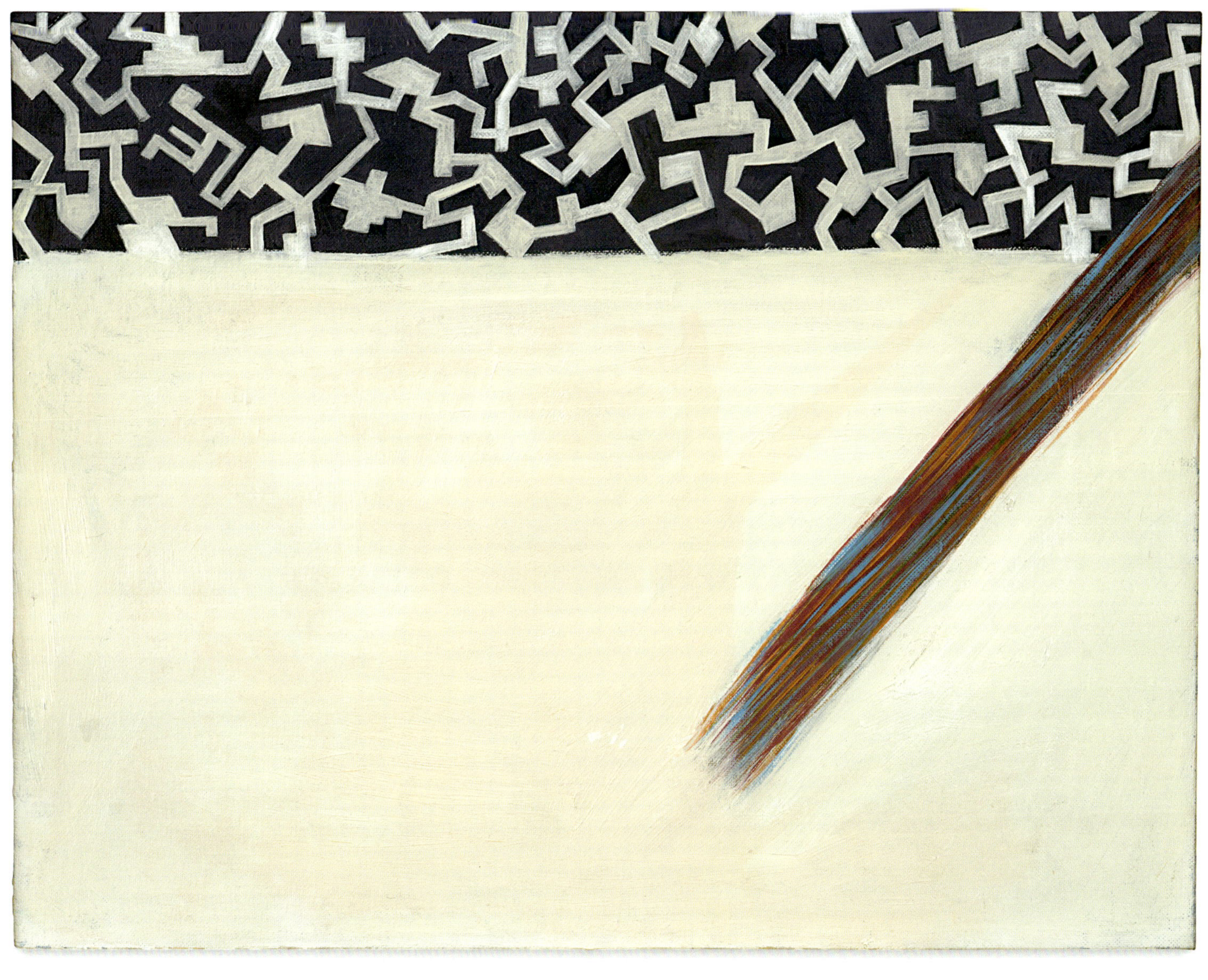

SPENT THE DAY IN THE BARN PAINTING... SOME INTERESTING WORK. THINGS SEEM TO BE GETTING BETTER—BUT STILL ODDLY TURNING SIMPLE— ONE IS VERY GOOD. IT IS VERY HARD TO WORK IN THIS FASHION.. .HEAVY DAYS THEN OFF A FEW DAYS... THEN ON AGAIN. STILL, THIS IS MUCH BETTER THAN A FEW MONTHS BACK.

JOURNAL ENTRY
Friday, August 29, 1980

LEFT IN THUNDERSTORM FOR CITY AT 2 AND MADE GOOD TIME. AT HOME—PHONE IS BROKEN. SPENT EVENING CLEANING HOUSE. ALSO: DRIVING HOME HAD AN IDEA ABOUT DOING BIG PICTURES... TO THINK OF REMBRANDT: COLOR, SHADOWS COME OFF OF A "THING" AND EXPAND TO FILL PIX. A STRUCTURE OF AIR, OF SHADOWS.

JOURNAL ENTRY
Monday, June 22, 1981

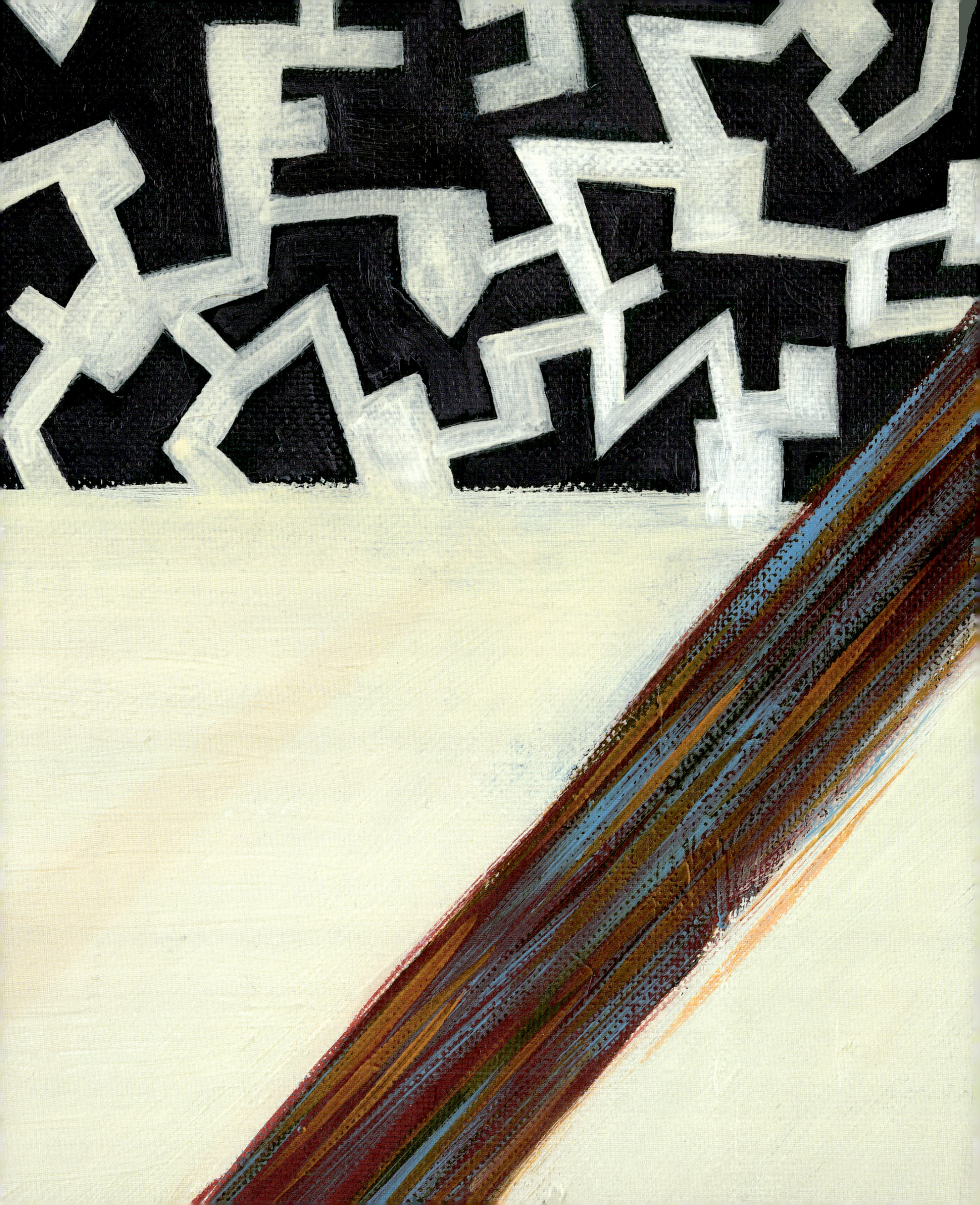

Untitled (4–14) 1982

oil on linen on panel
16 × 20"

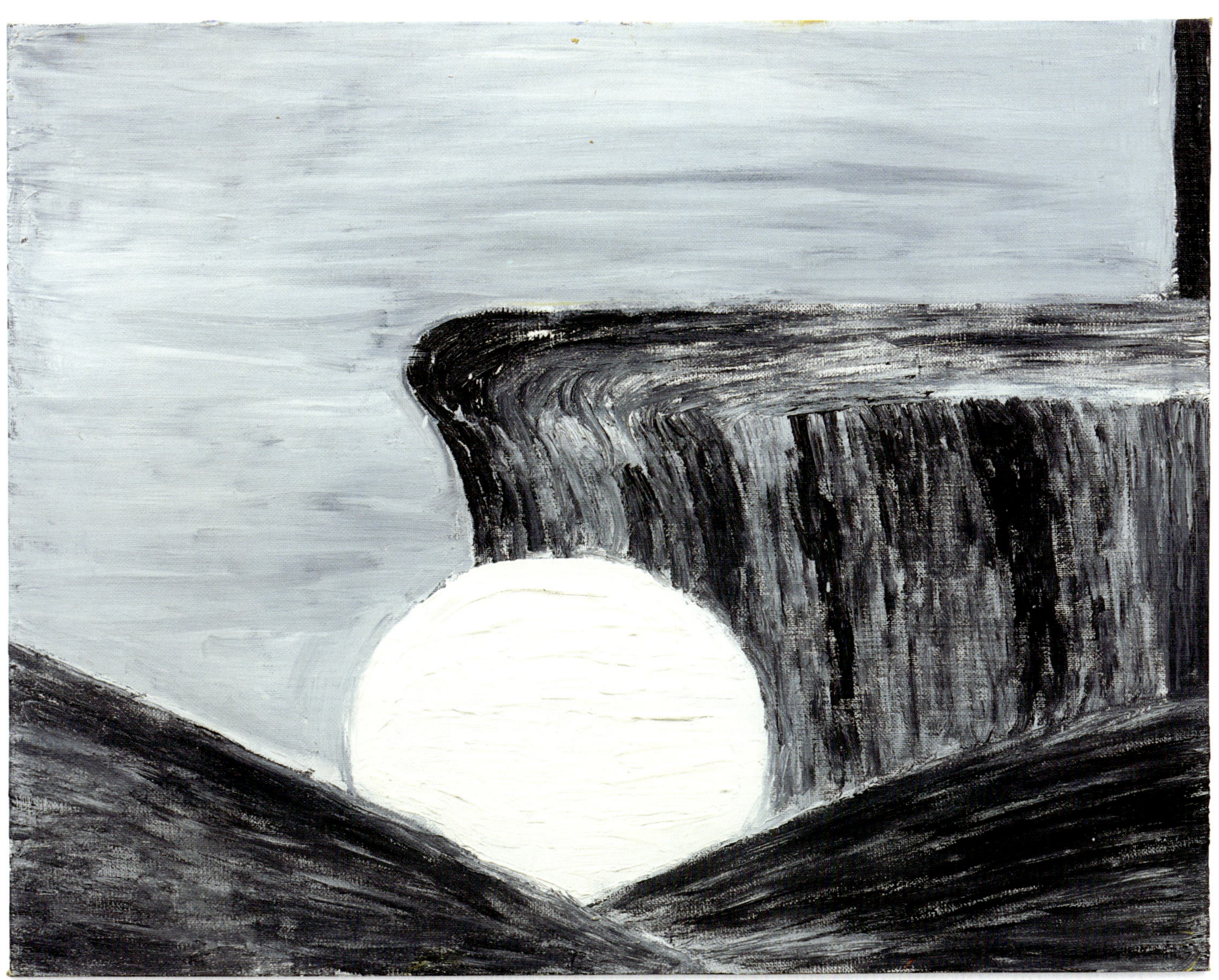

Untitled (2–55) 1982

oil on linen on panel
16 × 20"

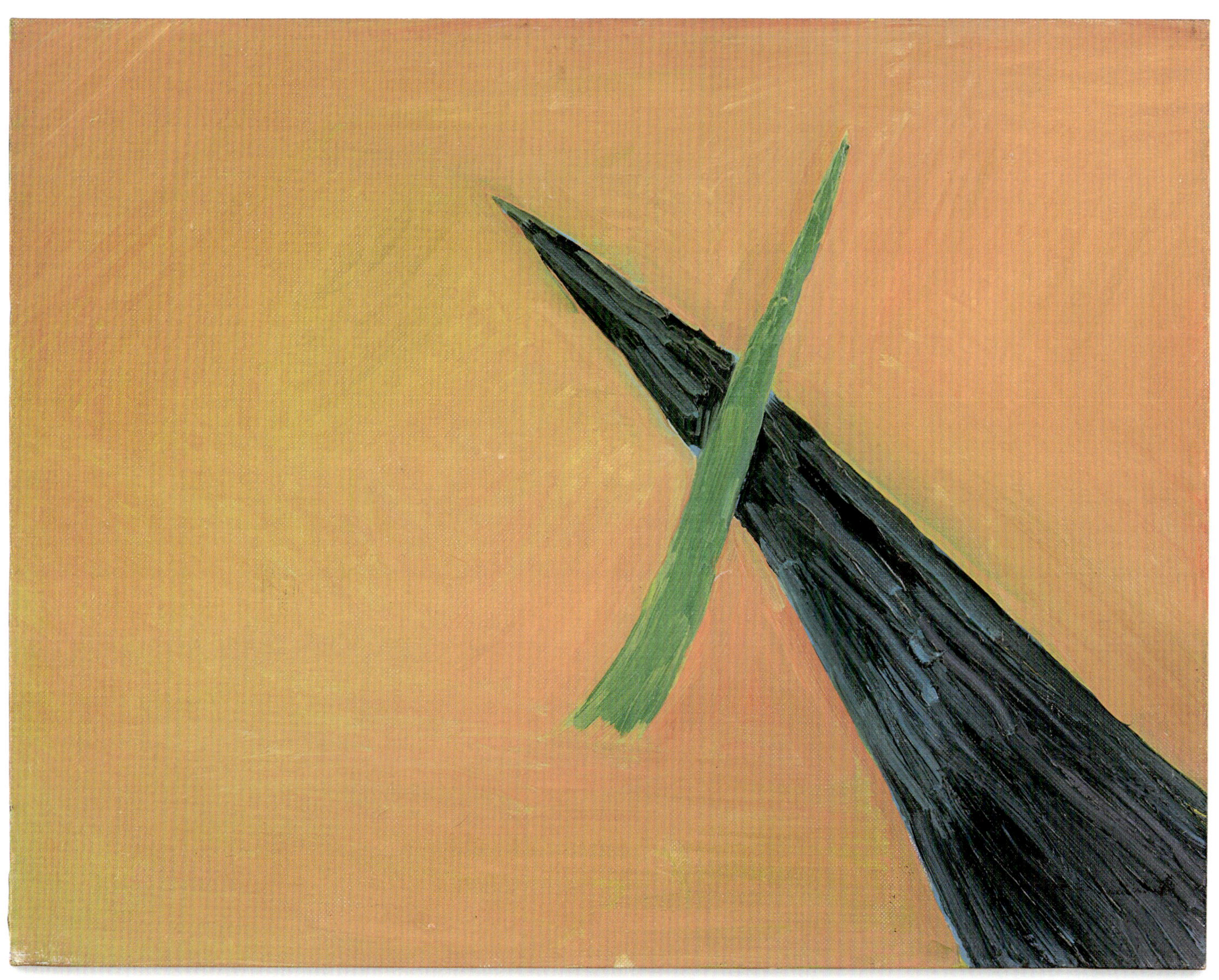

Untitled (4–67) 1983

oil on linen on panel
16 × 20"

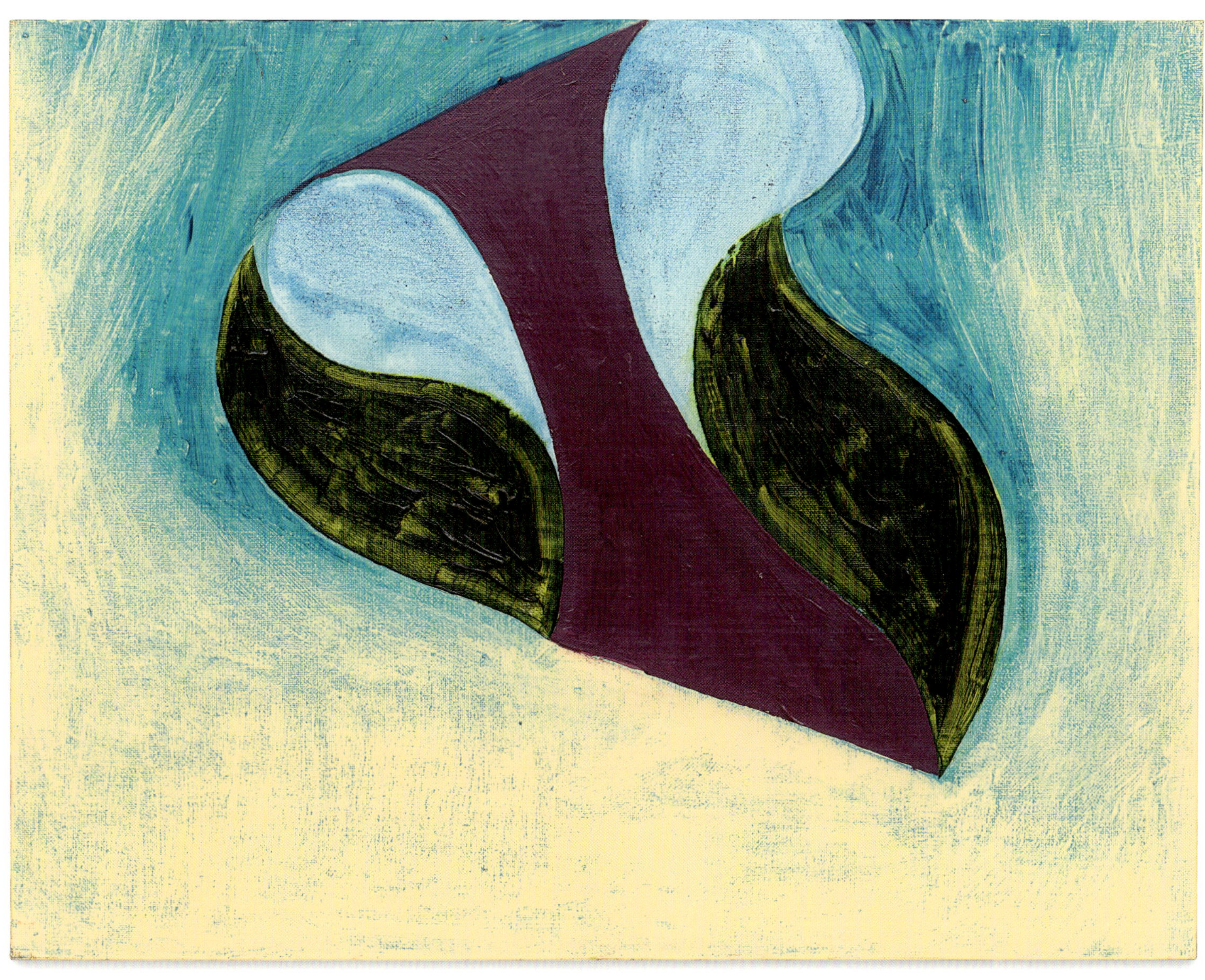

Untitled (4–113) 1986

oil on linen on panel
16 × 20"

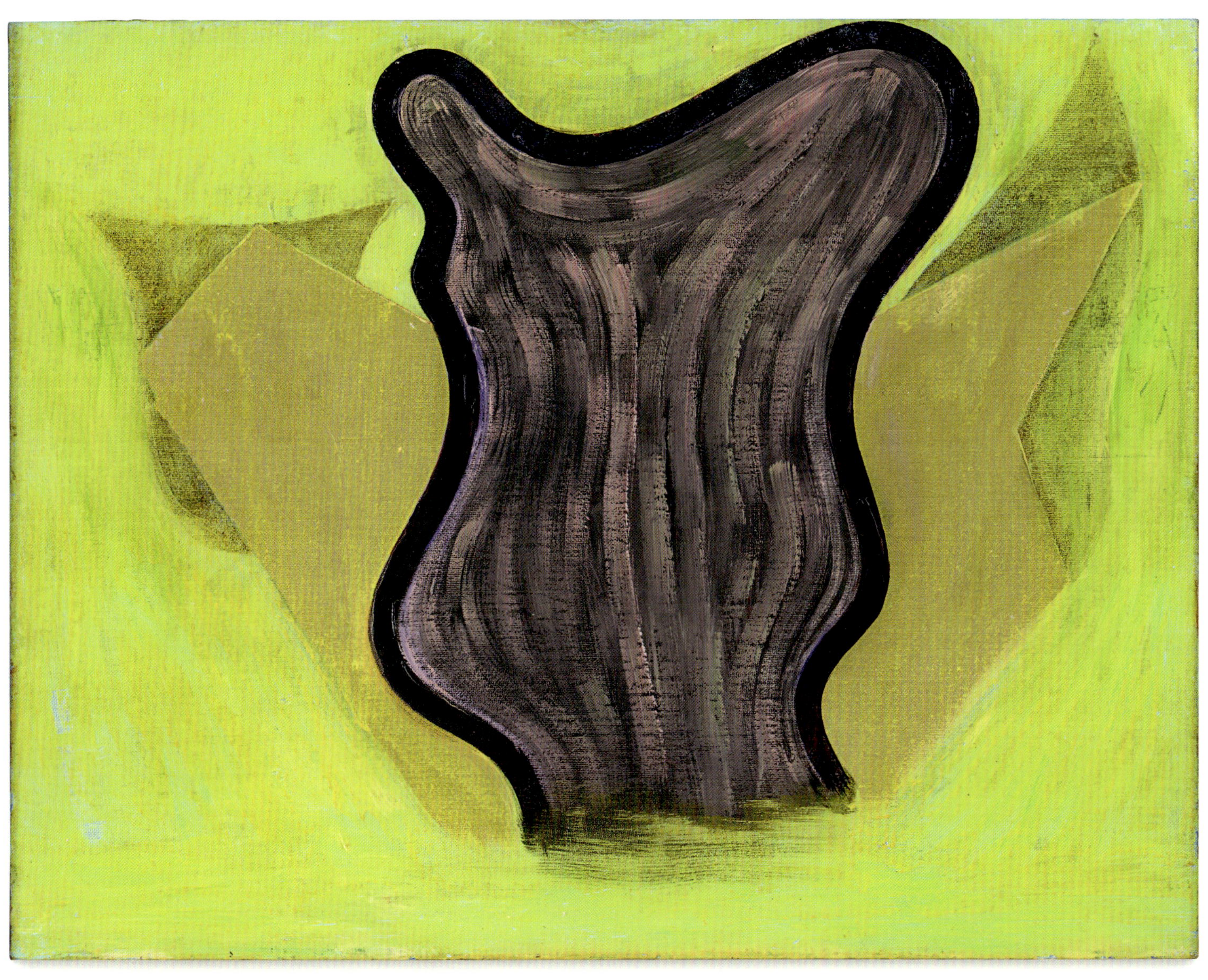

Untitled (4–120) 1986

oil on linen on panel
16 × 20"

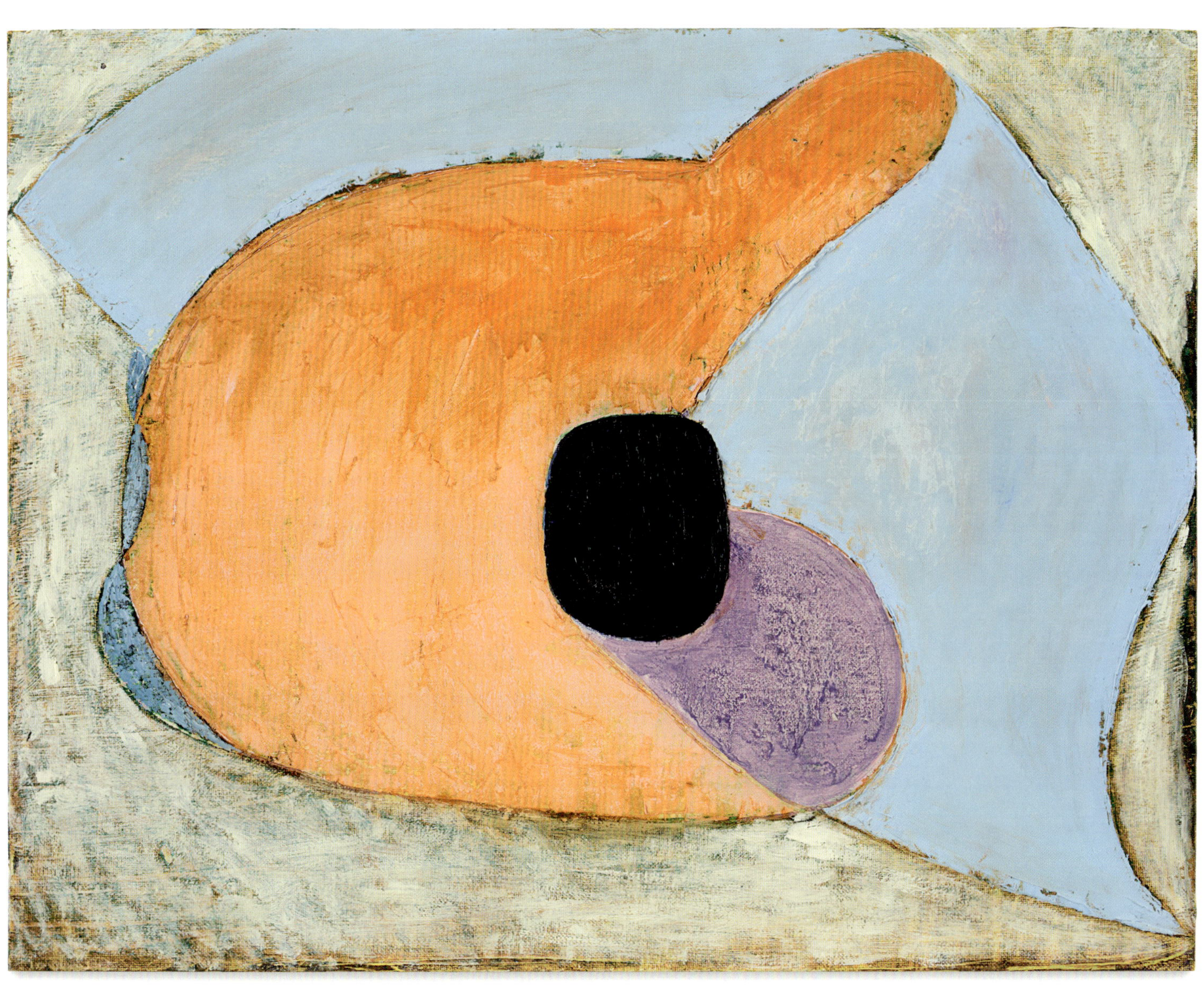

Untitled (6–10) 1986

oil on linen on panel
16 × 20"

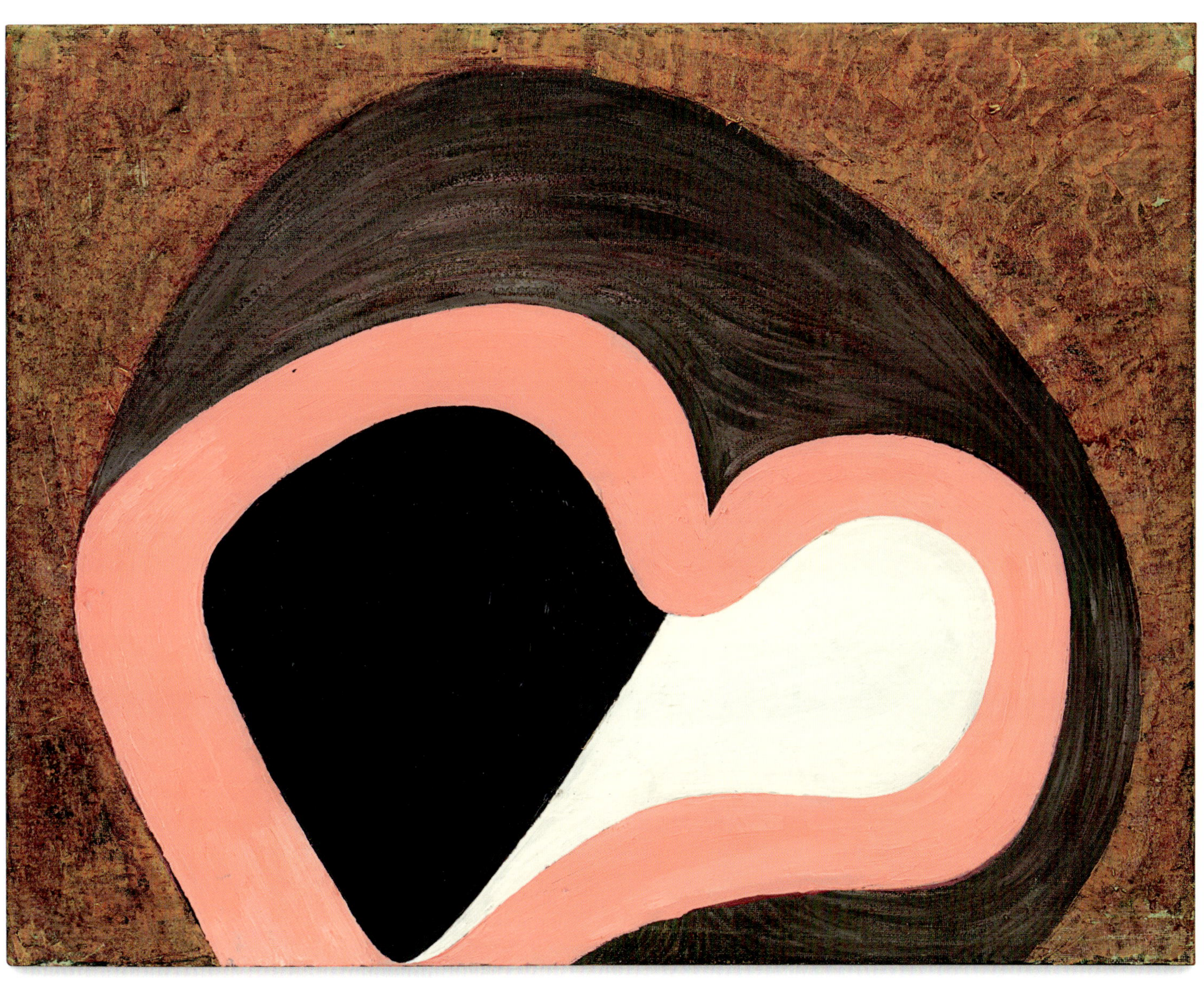

Untitled (6–11) 1986

oil on linen on panel
16 × 20"

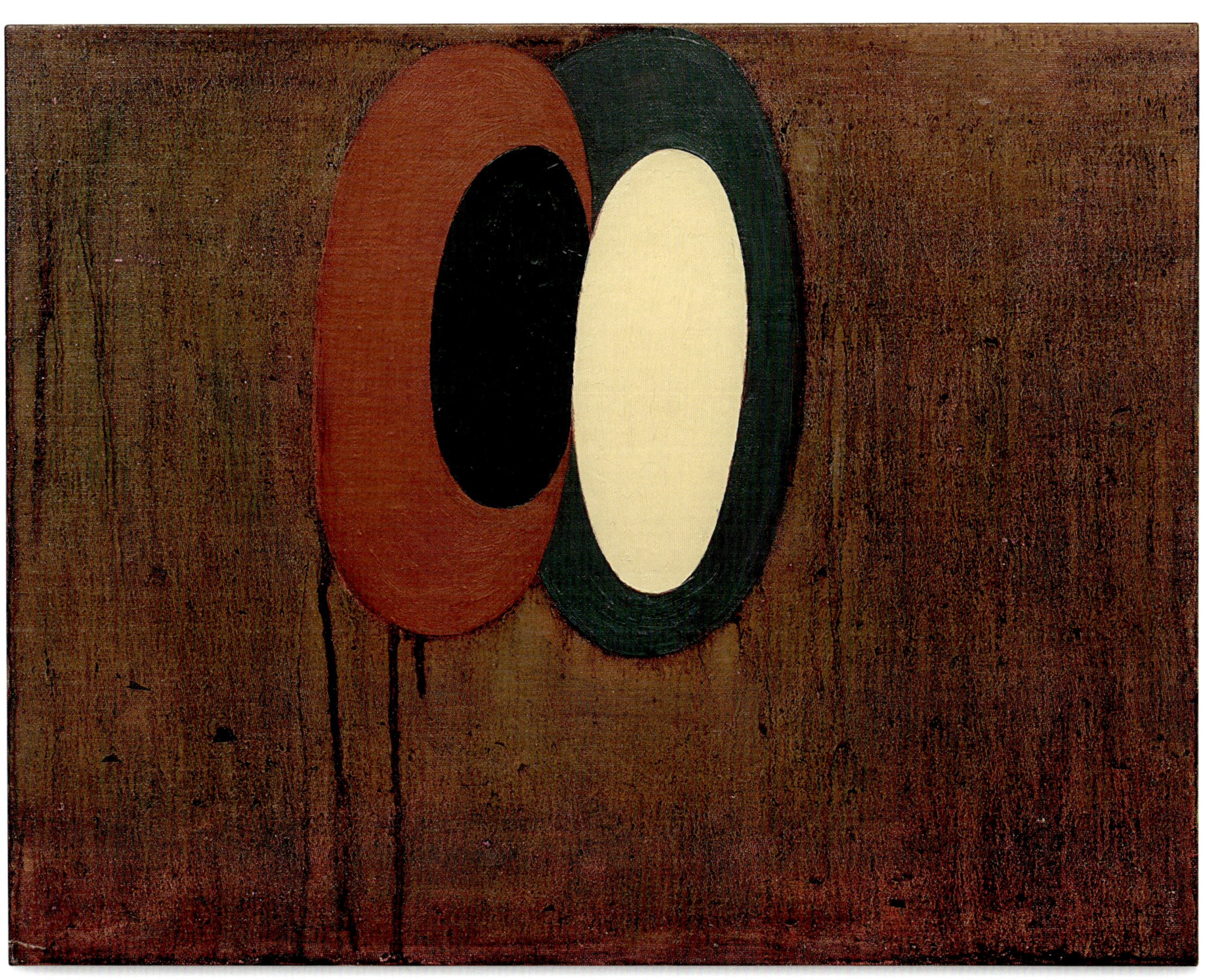

Untitled (6–36) 1987

oil on linen on panel

16 × 20"

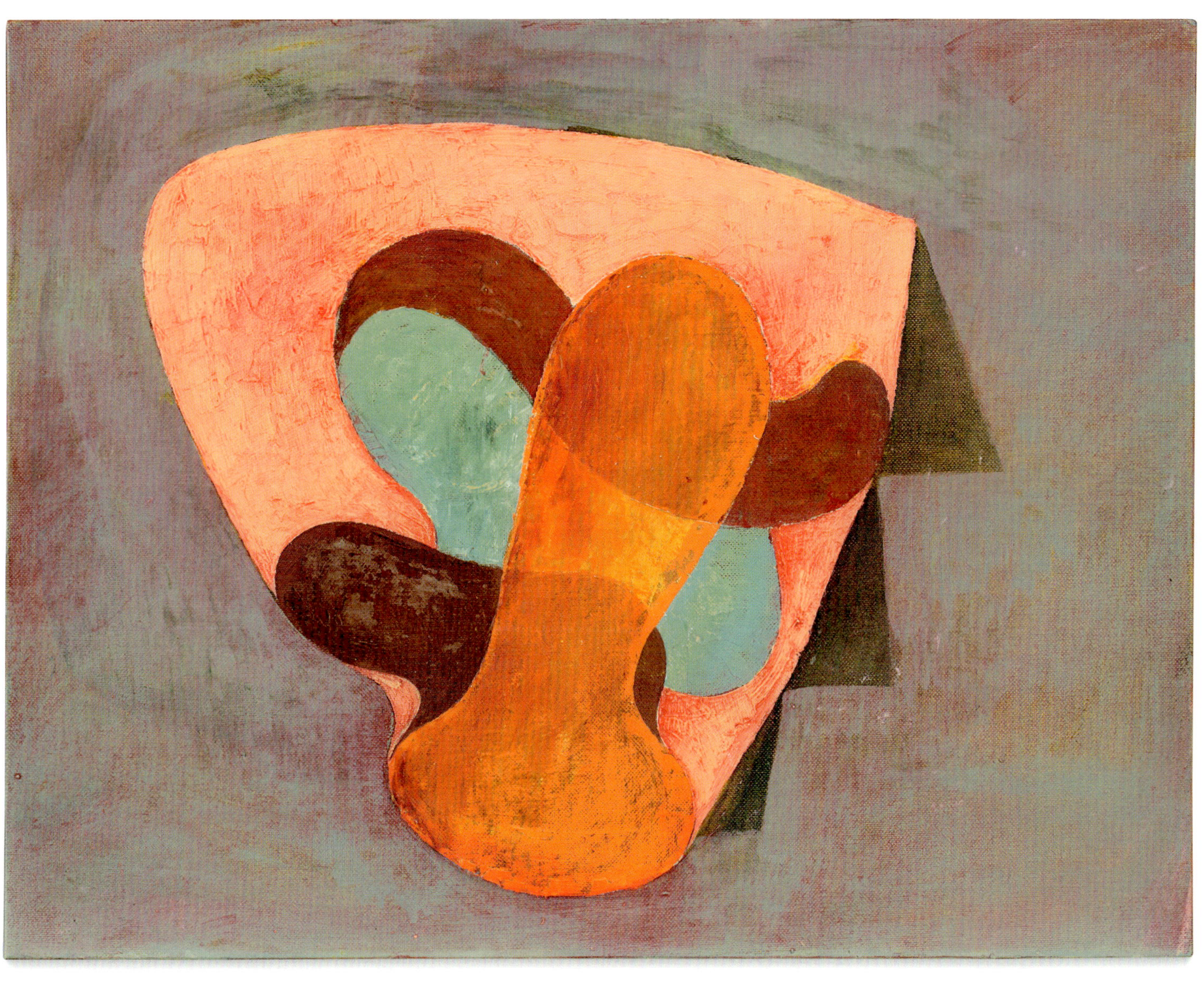

Untitled (6–61) 1988

oil on linen on panel
16 × 20"

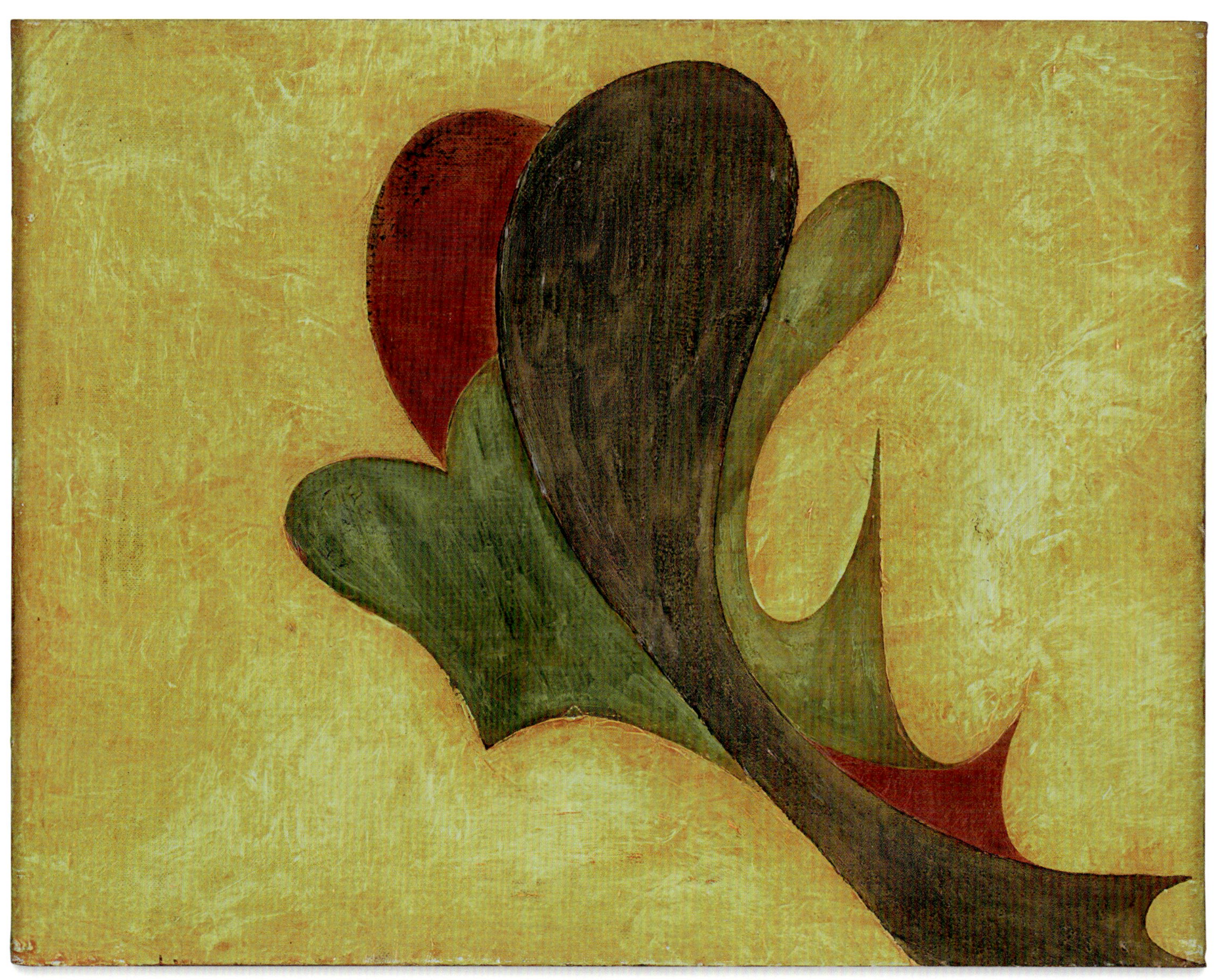

Untitled (8–79) c. 1990

oil on linen on panel
16 × 20"

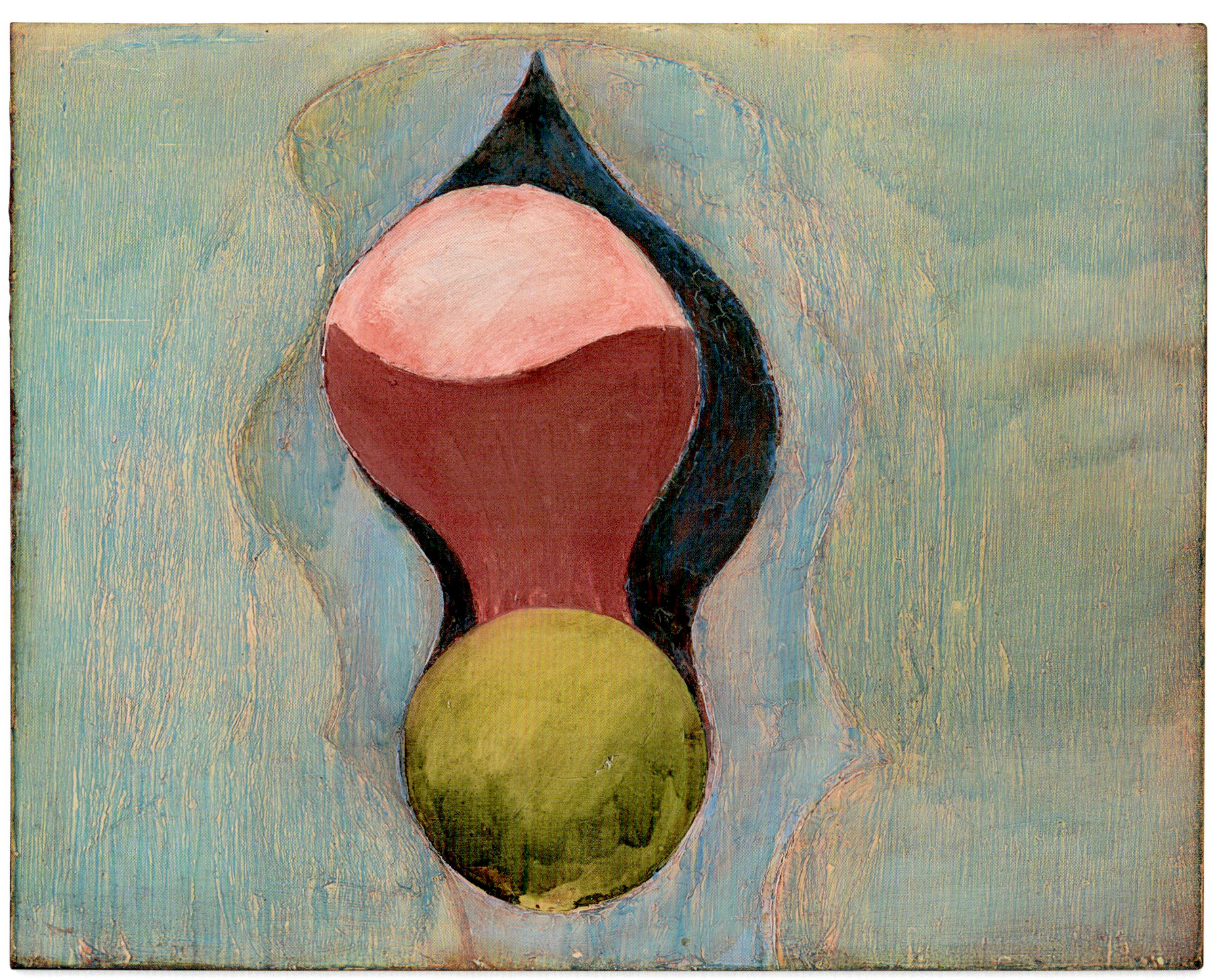

Untitled (6–16) 1991

oil on linen on panel
16 × 20"

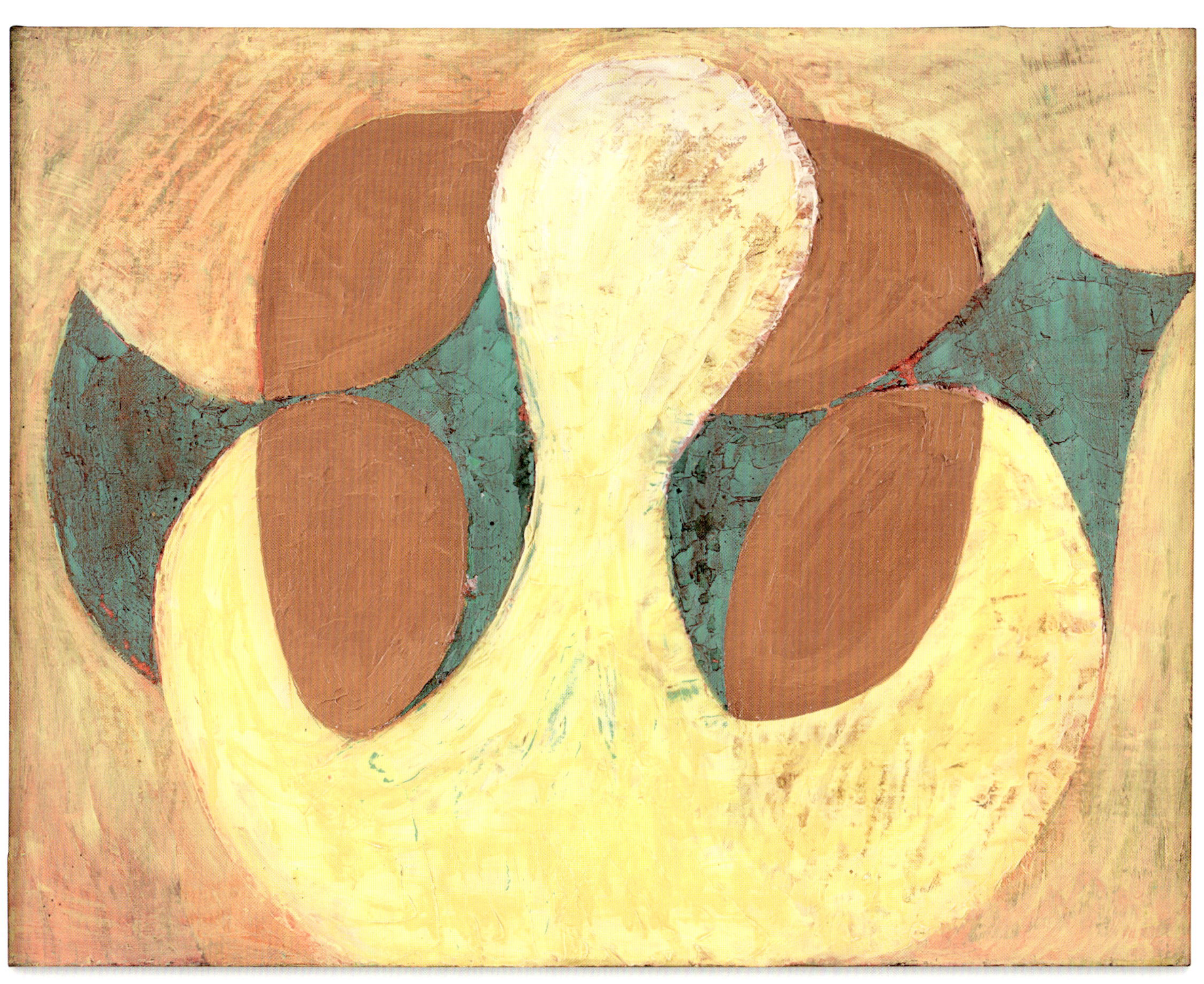

Untitled (LP–2) 1981

oil on linen on panel
50 1/8 × 60 1/2"

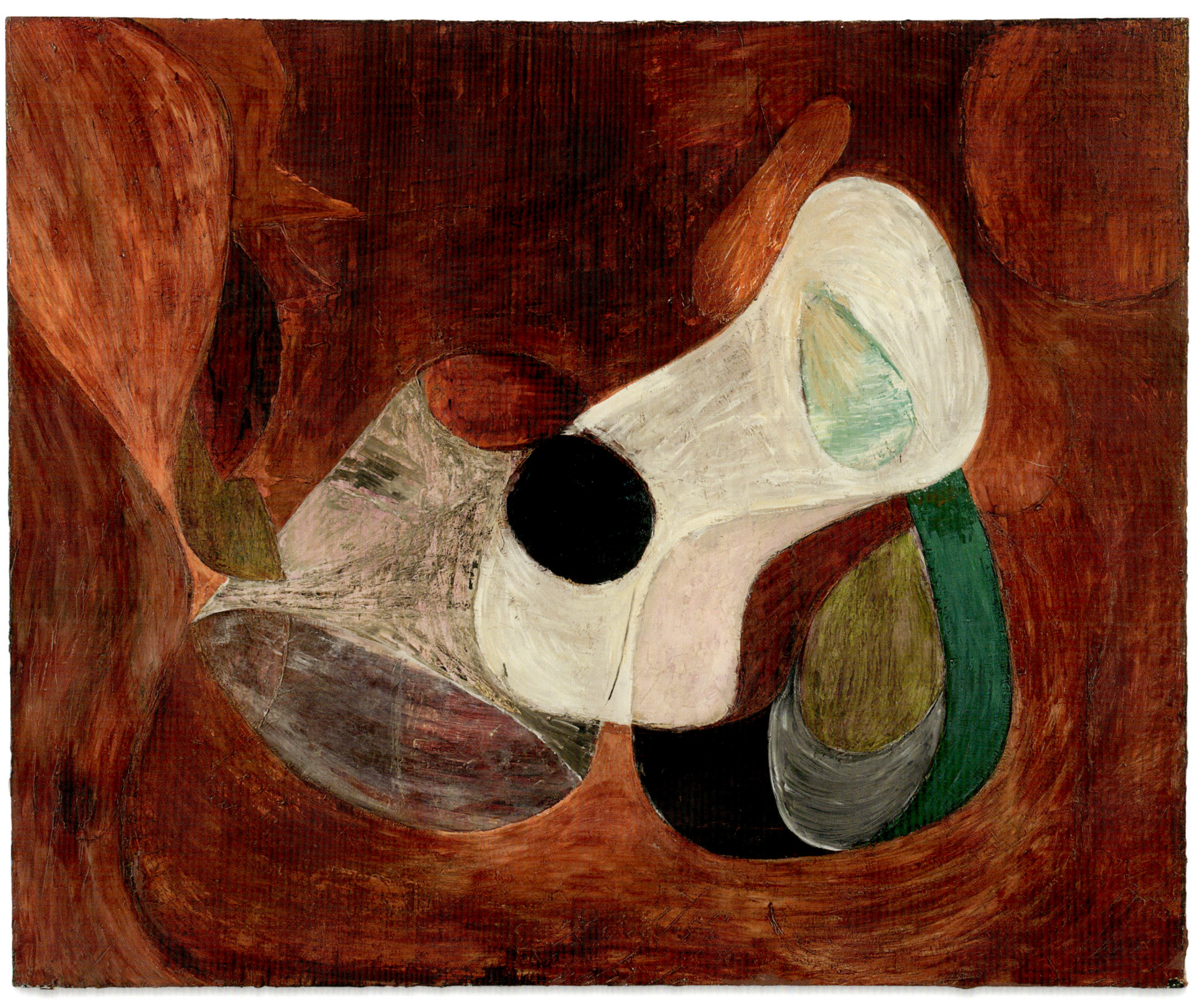

I FINALLY STARTED THE BIG 48X60 CANVAS. SKETCHED ON IT AND THINK I'LL DO SOMETHING ABOUT SEARCHING, SEARCHERS AND A DREAM I HAD ABOUT A LUMINOUS SQUARE FLOATING IN WATER AND MIRRORED IN THE SKY....

JOURNAL ENTRY
Sunday, August 2, 1981

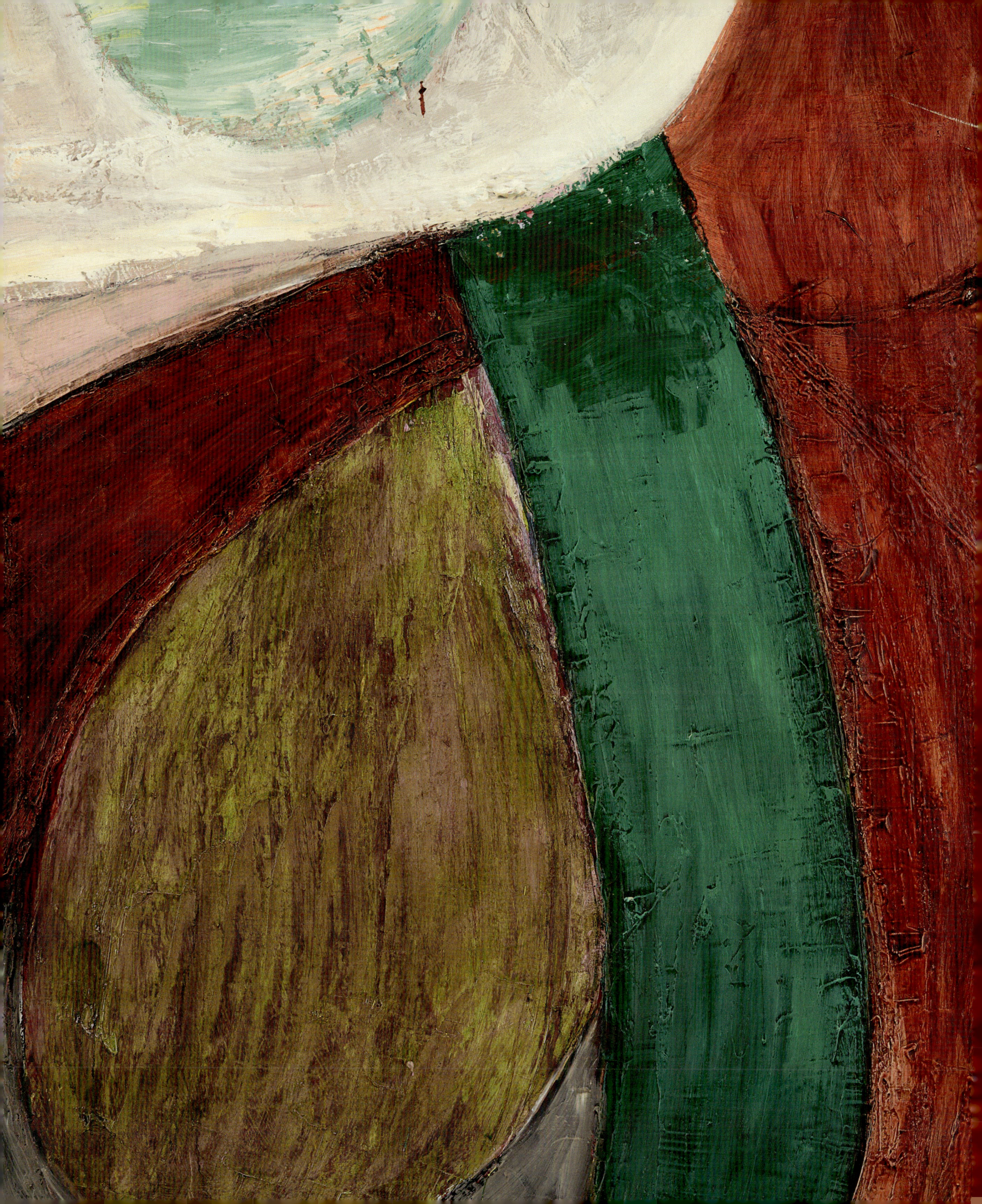

Untitled (LP–4) 1981–83

oil on linen on panel
48 ⅛ × 60 ¼"

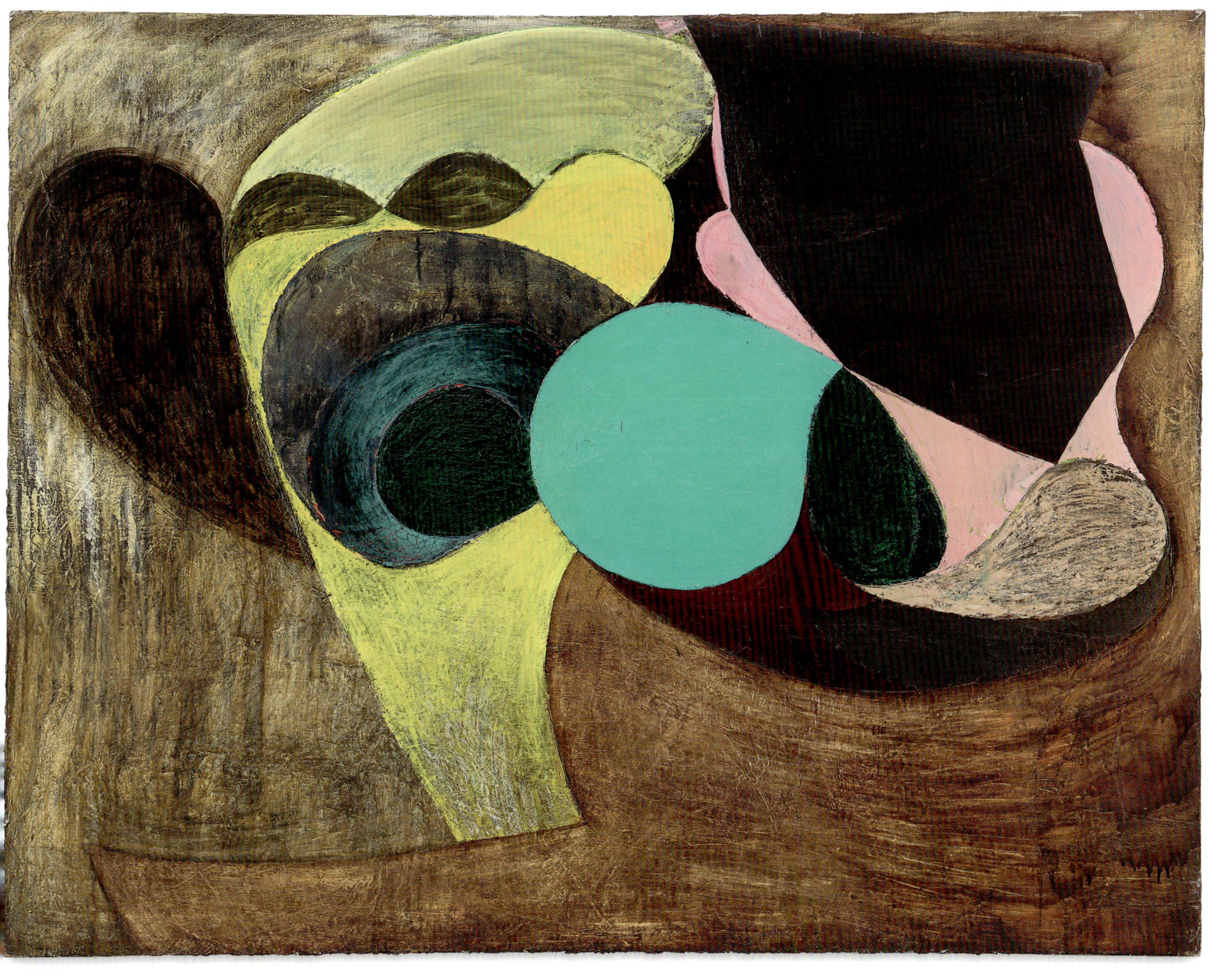

Untitled (LP–6) 1986

oil on linen on panel
48 × 60"

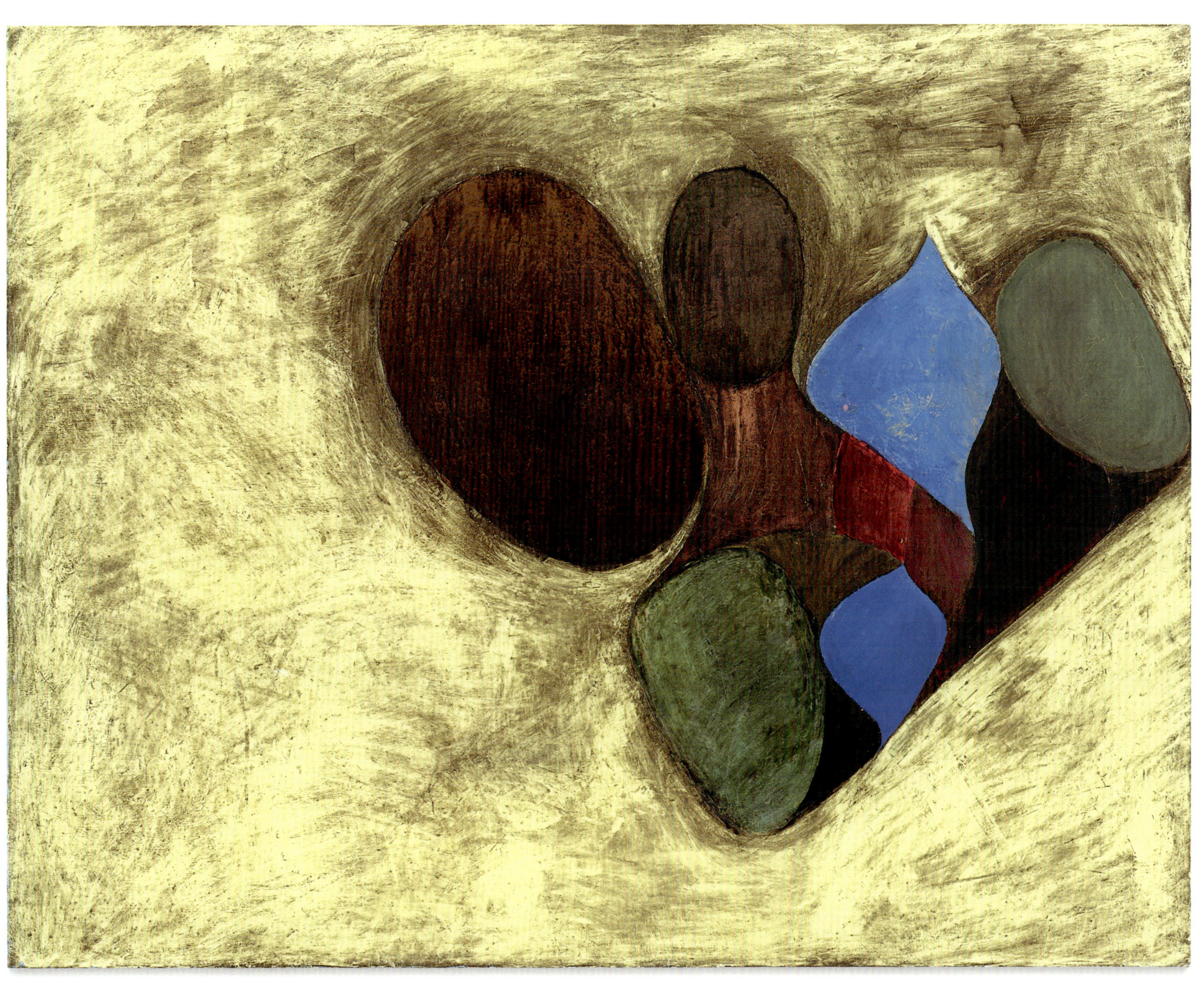

Untitled (LP-10) 1986

oil on linen on panel
48 × 60"

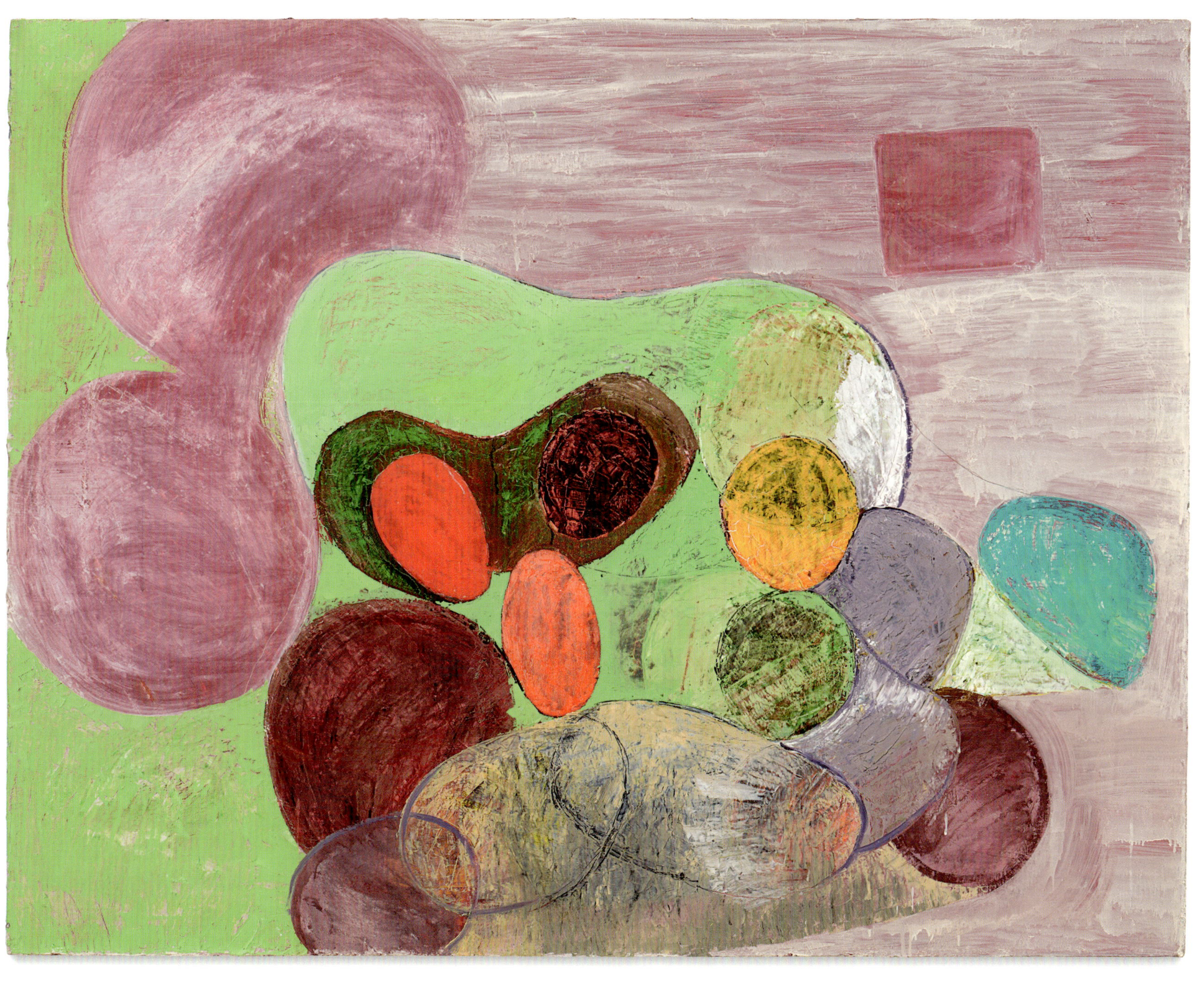

ANOTHER STRONG DAY OF PAINTING! THE KEY SEEMS TO LIE IN DOING FRESH WORK RATHER THAN CONTINUOUSLY BEATING HEAD AGAINST OLDER, UNFINISHED (MAYBE UNSOLVEABLE) PICTURES.

JOURNAL ENTRY
Monday, March 2, 1987

STOP AT AWOSTING FALLS. JUST A TRICKLE COMPARED TO HUGE THUNDERING WASH AFTER THE BIG RAINS IN EARLY SPRING.

JOURNAL ENTRY
Saturday, June 20, 1987

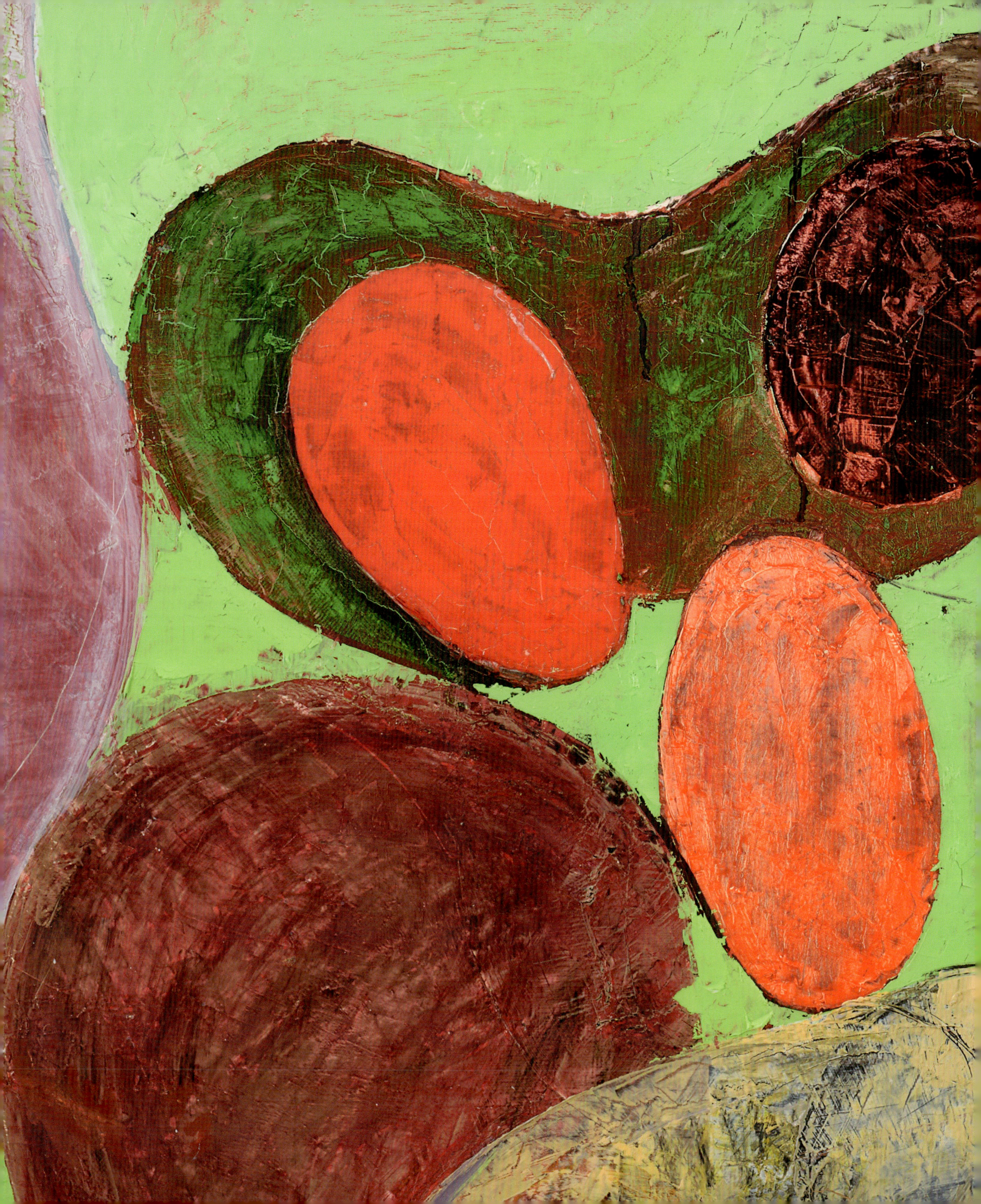

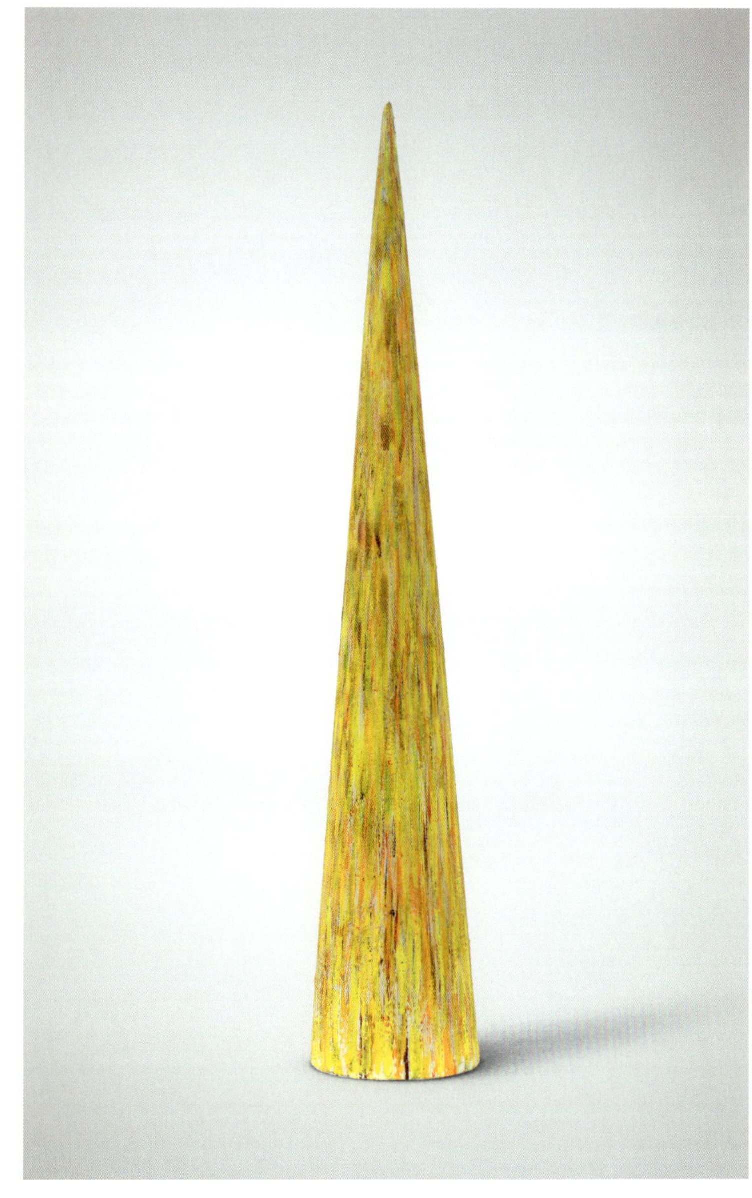

Untitled (CS-1) 1979

painted wood
approx. 30¾ × 5⅜ × 5¼"

Untitled (CS-2) 1979

painted wood
approx. 30¾ × 5⅜ × 5¼"

Untitled (CS-3) 1979

painted wood
approx. 30¾ × 5⅜ × 5¼"

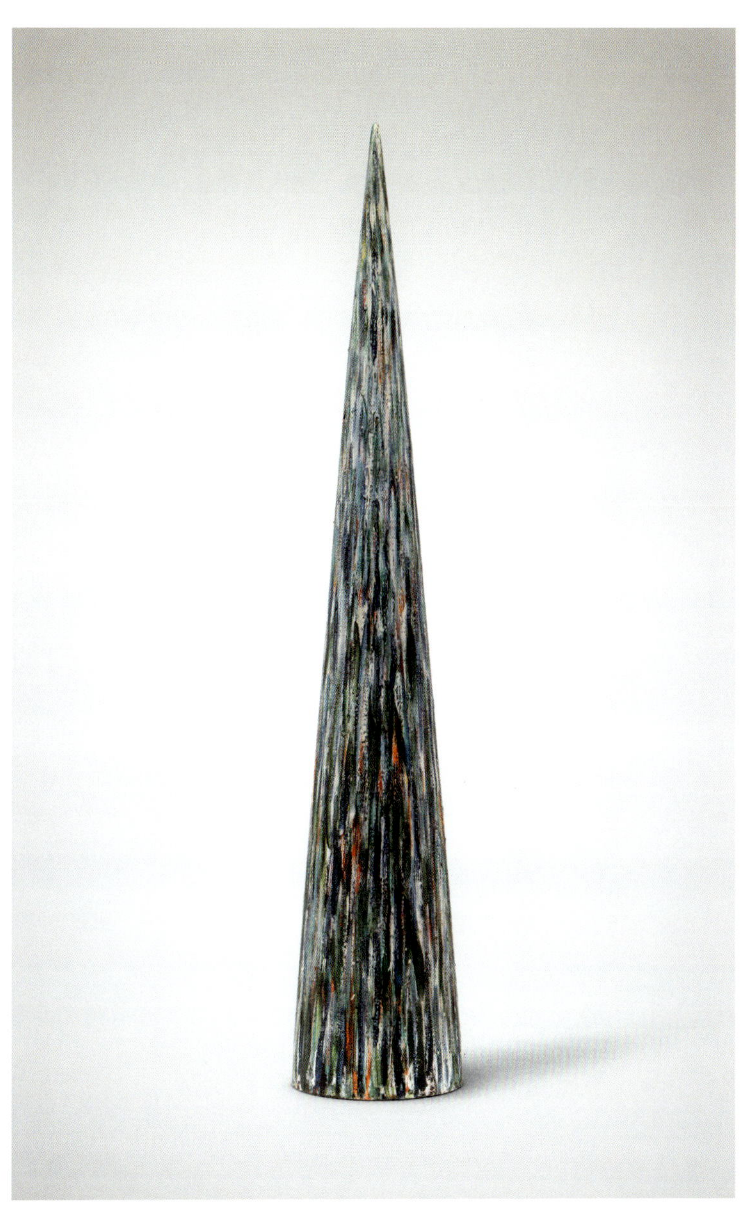

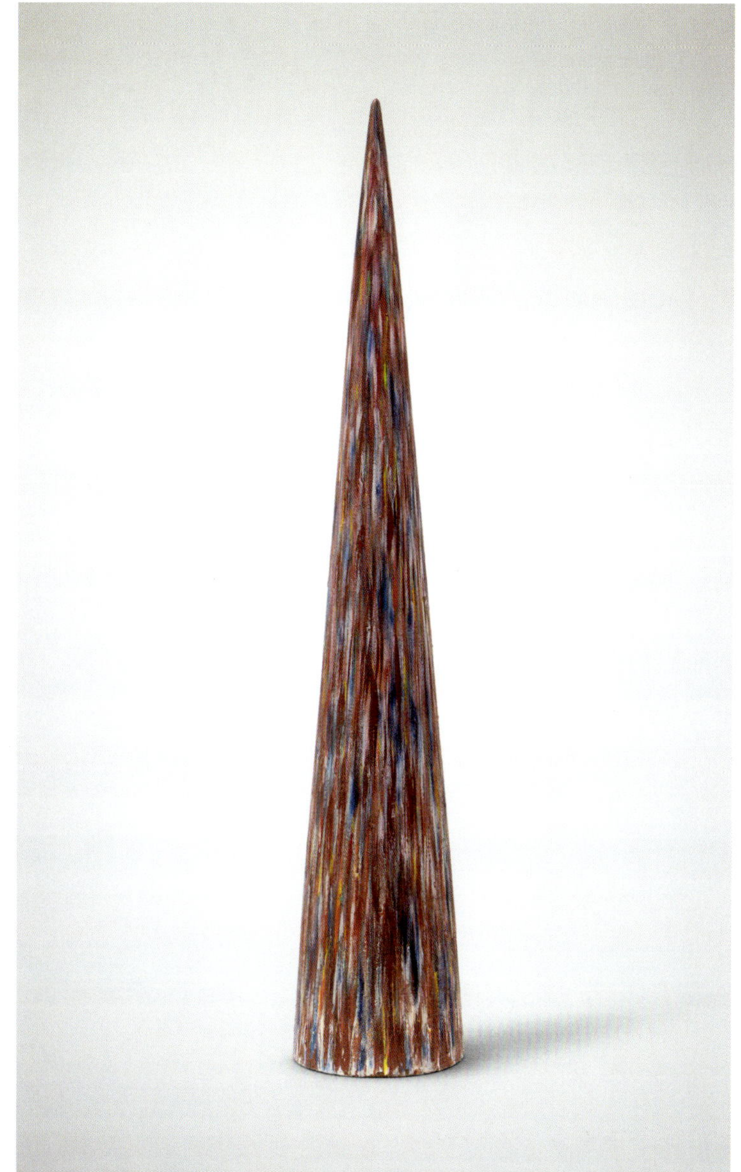

List of Works

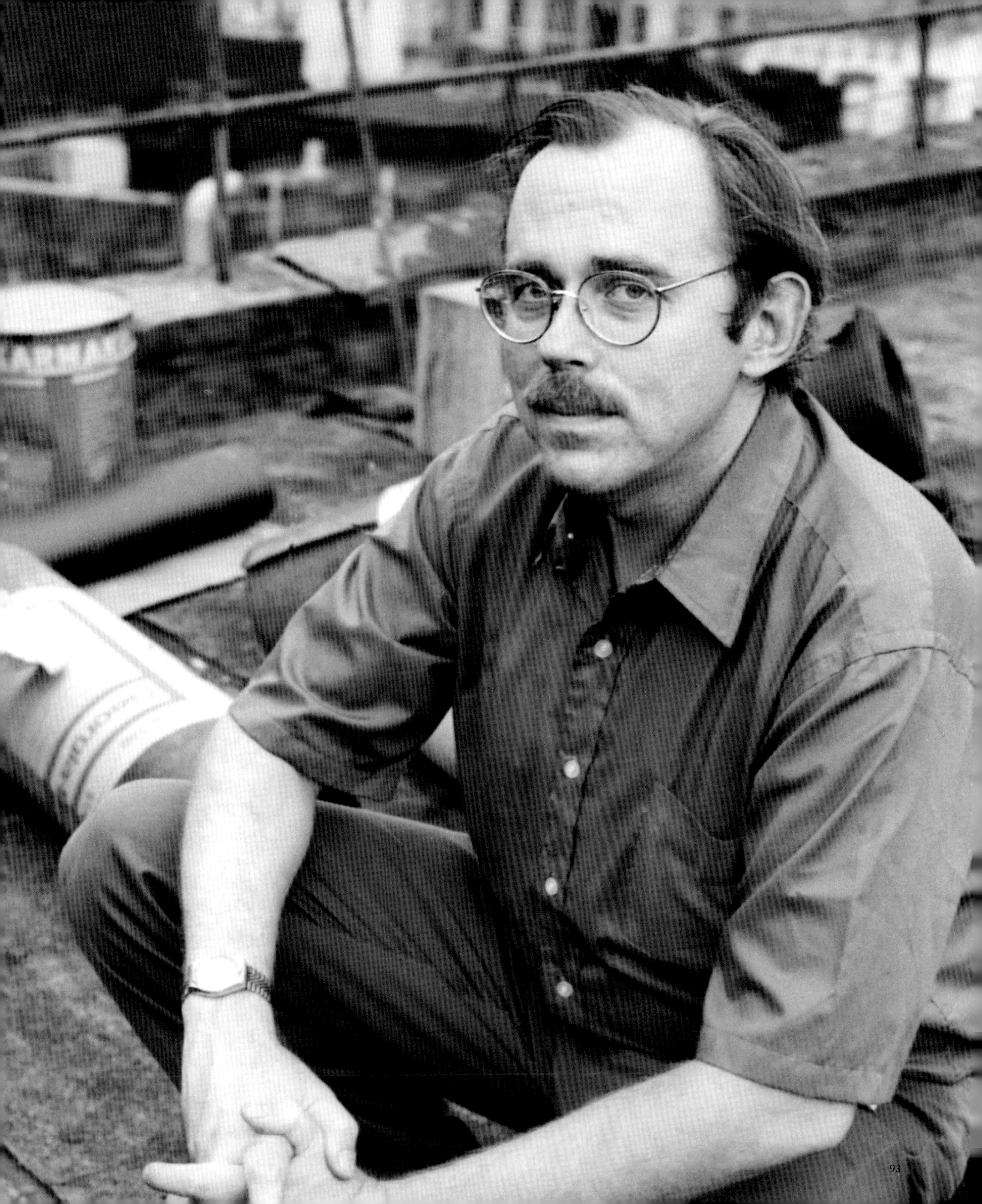

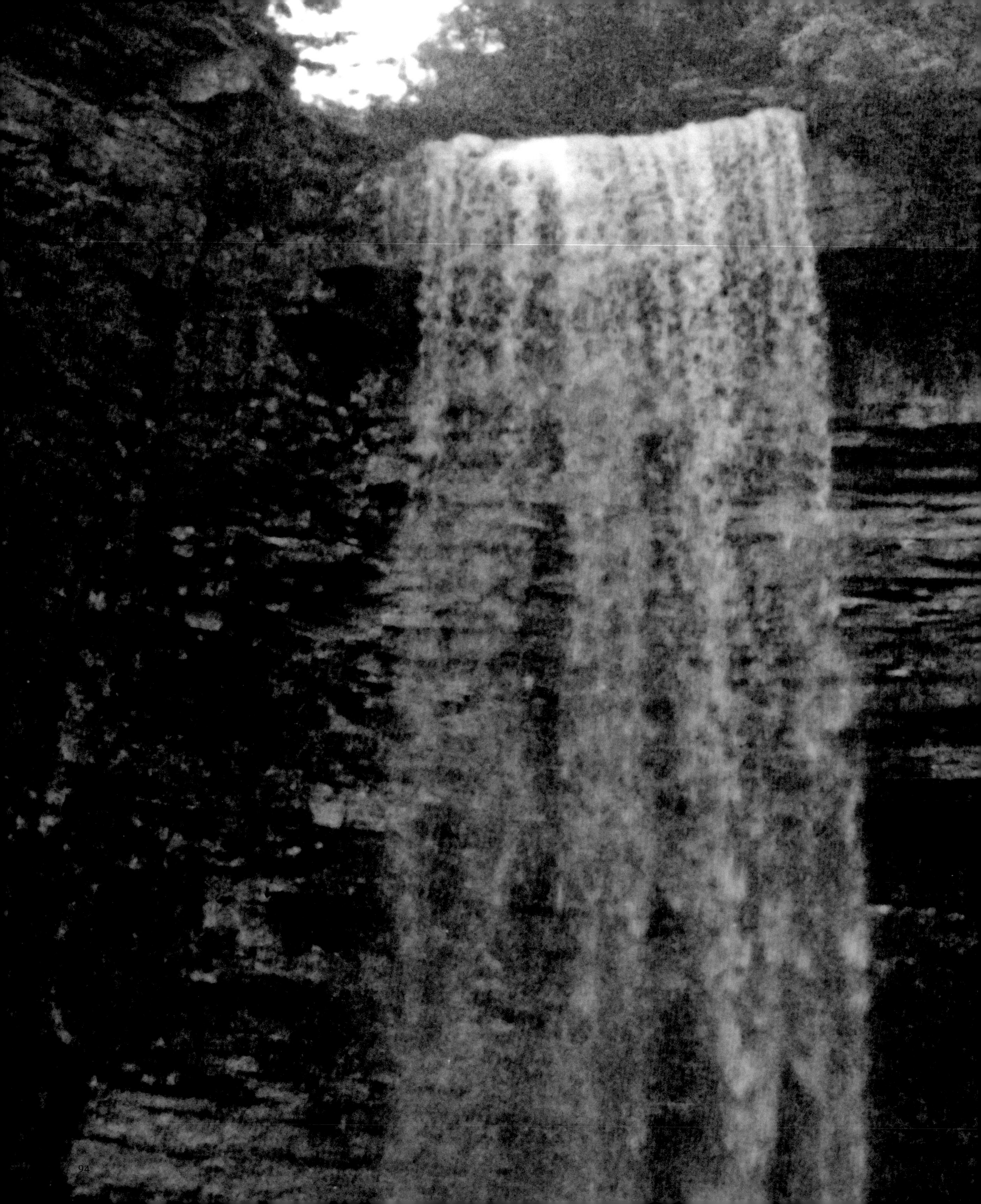

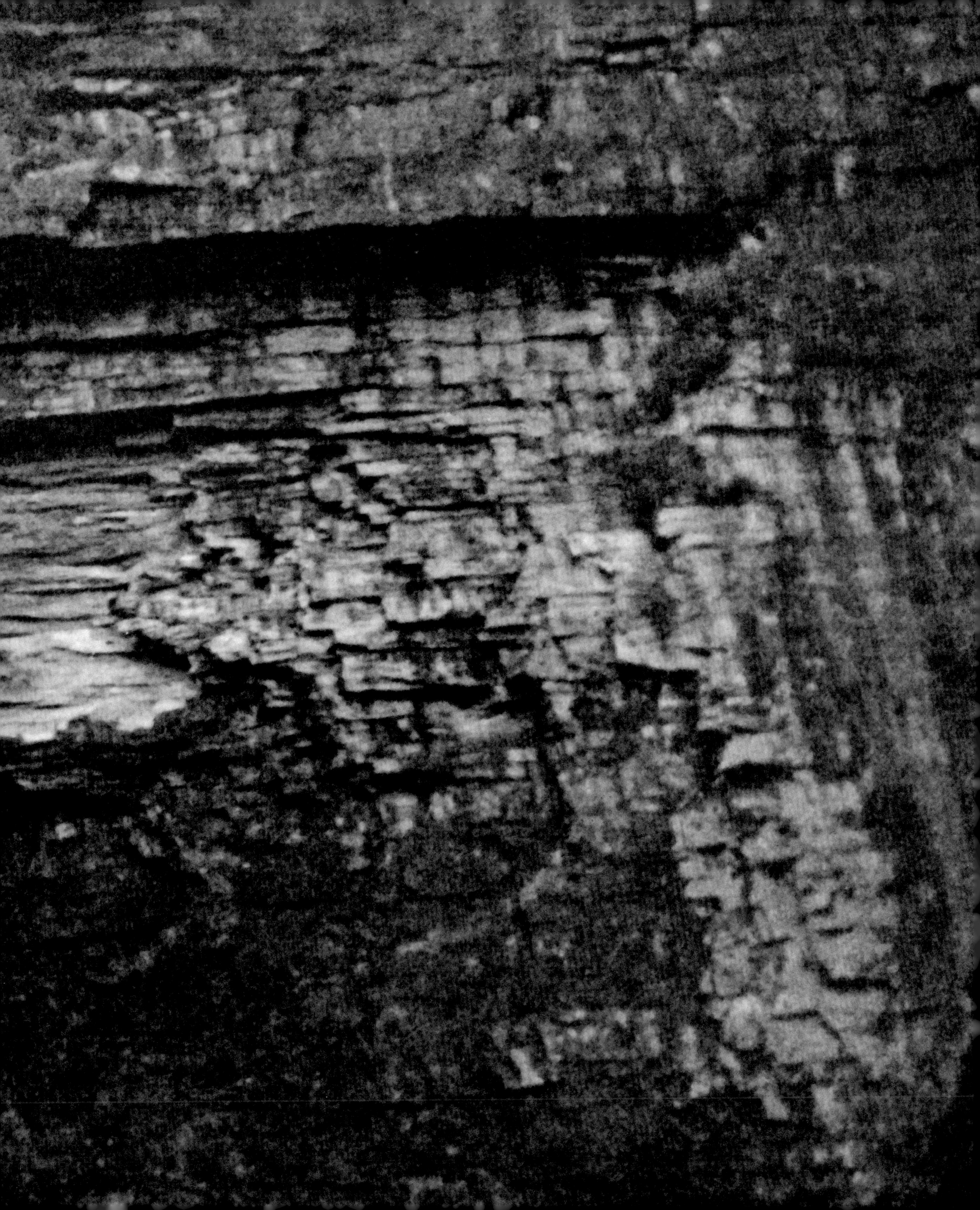

Published on the occasion of
Thomas Nozkowski: Everything in the World
March 8 – April 20, 2024

Pace Gallery
540 West 25th Street
New York

Cover: Thomas Nozkowski, *Untitled (LP-10)*, 1986 (detail)
pp. 94–95: Stony Kill Falls, Wawarsing, New York. Photo by Thomas Nozkowski

Photography:
G.R. Christmas: p. 47
Peter Clough: pp. cover, 23, 25, 27, 29, 31, 33, 37, 39, 41, 43, 45, 49, 51, 53, 55, 57, 59, 61, 63, 65, 67, 69, 71, 73, 75, 77, 79, 81, 83, 85, 87, 89, 90–91
Kerry Ryan McFate: p. 35
© The Museum of Modern Art / Licensed by SCALA / Art Resource, NY: pp. 16 (fig. 3), 19 (fig. 5)
Thomas Nozkowski: pp. 2–3, 13 (fig. 1), 94–95
Pace Gallery: p. 6
Photographer Andrea Rossetti / Fridericianum, Kassel: p. 19 (fig. 4)
Kunié Sugiura: p. 93
© Tate, London / Art Resource, NY: p. 19 (fig. 6)
Earl Willis, Nobe Gallery: p. 13 (fig. 2)

Creative Director: Tomo Makiura
Design: Tara Stewart
Production: Paul Pollard
Editorial Manager: Sara Harrison
Editorial: Madeline Gilmore
Rights & Reproductions: Vincent Wilcke
Color Separations: Altaimage, New York

Printing: Meridian Printing, East Greenwich, Rhode Island
Typeset in William Subhead and William Text

ISBN: 978-1-948701-68-6
Library of Congress Control Number: 2024930553

Available through ARTBOOK | D.A.P.
75 Broad Street, Suite 630 New York, NY 10004
www.artbook.com